Picardy

An Australian garden inspired by a passion for all things French

Marian Somes

Picardy

An Australian garden inspired by
a passion for all things French

Marian Somes

echo

This book is for Bryce and my family
Genevieve, Steve and Thomas
Nicholas, Judy, Charlie and Carrie
Anna, Duncan, Angus, Lachlan and Maisie

A division of Bonnier Publishing Australia
534 Church Street, Richmond
Victoria Australia 3121
www.echopublishing.com.au

First published 2018
Printed in China
Cover design by Tracy Loughlin
Cover image © Sue Stubbs
Page design and typesetting by Tracy Loughlin
Photography by Sue Stubbs
Every attempt has been made to trace and acknowledge copyright for the images. Where an attempt has been unsuccessful, the publisher would be pleased to hear from the copyright owner so any omission or error can be rectified.
Typeset in Brandon Grotesque
A catalogue entry for this book is available from the National Library of Australia.
ISBN: 9781760680541 (hardback).

bonnierpubau
@bonnierpublishingau
@bonnierpublishingau

contents

The French obsession

Why this obsession with France? In 1986, after years of reading about France, trying to learn to speak French, and cooking and eating French food, we finally decided to celebrate a landmark birthday year by visiting the country itself. A fluent French-speaking English friend offered to take us as passengers on his regular business trip, calling on several regions throughout the country.

After spending a few days in London sightseeing and recovering from jetlag we met up with our friend and travelled to Dover. From there we crossed the English Channel by ferry to Calais. Within minutes of arriving on French soil, while driving from the ferry terminal along a busy thoroughfare and craning my neck to get my first glimpses of the country, we came across the ridiculous sight of an angry moustachioed comic-strip Frenchman, wearing a pith helmet with a feather cockade, voluminous shorts and gaiters, and riding a banana-coloured tricycle in and out of the heavy Calais afternoon traffic. Pedalling like crazy he pulled out in front of a coach emblazoned with the Union Jack and full of English tourists. He held up his hand to halt the coach and gesticulated in no uncertain terms that they should return from whence they had come. It was like being on a Jacques Tati film set. How happy he would be with the Brexit result!

This episode set the tone for the rest of our whistle-stop tour. I was expecting the French to be different, and I wasn't disappointed.

That night we stayed in Amiens, a major city in Picardy, with an awe-inspiring cathedral. In an unpretentious little restaurant I ate my first genuine *coq au vin*. I remember the pretty, shy waitress with her beautiful soft accent. The next day our road trip began in earnest, and we drove to Versailles. It was a Saturday morning – market day. It was spring, the season for the white asparagus which was sold in fat bundles tied with red, white and blue ribbon stamped with the name of the grower. Strawberries nestled in little wooden punnets lined with their own fresh green leaves. Plump cheeses, filling the air with pungent scents, lay on straw mats. Fish glistened on beds of ice, their scales shining like sequins. Our appetites whetted, we lunched at the restaurant Chapeau Gris, a bustling traditional *bistrot*. The waiters in long aprons sashayed around, plates of *bifsteak*

et frites held high. Napkins were unfurled with a flourish and our orders listened to as if they were the most interesting news heard all day – truly a *tour de force* performance!

Our accommodation for the weekend was L'hotel Trianon. *C'est vraiment magnifique* – the side gate opened into the gardens of the Palace of Versailles. Early Sunday morning, after a breakfast of perfect croissants served in a glass-walled orangerie, we walked around the gardens admiring the magnificent fountains, the grand *allées* of trees bordering long canals. Truly breathtaking – but the area that I loved best were the gardens around the fairy-tale farmhouse to which Marie Antoinette escaped when the rigours of the Court became too much for her.

Later we drove into the beautiful Normandy countryside for lunch at a charming country restaurant. I particularly remember the pale-pink damask napery, the *poule aux morilles* and the stunning dessert of strawberries baked in a puff-pastry case – and if that wasn't enough we then visited the Impressionist artist Monet's garden at Giverny. This garden and its pretty pink house would become a glorious inspiration. The geometric formal gardens in front of the house overflowed with roses and flowers in a stunning profusion of colour and perfume. The perfect juxtaposition of control and abandonment.

Monday morning saw us whipping along the Périphérique into Paris and our first glimpse of the Eiffel Tower. Our 'chauffeur' had business to attend to so we became *flâneurs* and spent the day strolling around the city. We walked and walked, admiring the beautiful balconied buildings, their window boxes filled with bright geraniums. We goggled at the gorgeous *chocolateries* and *pâtisseries* with their window displays like jewellery boxes: rows of identical *petit gateaux* and *tartes*, each one a tiny work of art. Elegant women in pastel-coloured spring outfits wafted faint perfumes as they passed, and dogs with their owners promenaded. Cafés bustled, their street-side cane chairs all facing outwards so as to view the passing parade, and all around us the gentle cadences of the language ... a feast for the senses. Late afternoon it began to rain and the streets were colour-washed with reflected lights and suddenly filled with black umbrellas as Parisians raced for the Métro or, like us, found an agreeable little bar to shelter in. Our bar was a postcard cliché. Zinc counter, dark wood panelling, rows of glistening glass bottles filled with rainbow-coloured liqueurs and syrups, black bentwood chairs and small round tables, windows streaked with raindrops and all overhung with a smoky fug. Heaven.

Our next brief stop was at Beaune in Burgundy. Our hotel was furnished with country antiques and provincial fabrics. Just around the corner was the *Hôtel-*

Dieu with a fantastic roof of green and yellow fishscale tiles. Unfortunately we were not here long enough to visit the famous vineyards, but we did manage to savour the wine at dinner.

The three of us continued on our way to Belfort, an industrial town where we ate in a tiny little black-walled restaurant the size of a shoebox. A young woman appeared to be the *patronne*, chef, *serveuse* and *sommelière*. She cooked and served us the most delicious pigeon. From there we went to Alsace, to Ribeauville, a chocolate-box village of coloured houses with heart shapes cut into the shutters and a distinctly Teutonic feel. *Choucroute*, the most famous regional dish, was on the menu at our chosen brasserie. Mine was served with an erect pig's tail as a garnish, and from the sniggers coming from the kitchen I think false assumptions had been made about our relationships.

Our last night was in Épernay in the Champagne region. Every holiday should end with champagne.

This first flying visit to France ignited our lifelong passion for French food, architecture and style. We have returned to France five times since that first whirlwind trip and have visited wonderful gardens and impressive *châteaux*, rented homely *gîtes* and gorgeous houses, stayed in quaint *chambre d'hôtes* and barged down canals. We have spent Christmas in Paris in a tiny apartment on the Île St-Louis and stayed in small picturesque villages in the countryside.

Coco Chanel is reputed to have said, 'My life didn't please me, so I created my life.' Our house and garden, which we have made together, is our attempt to create a little taste of France at home in Australia.

1 Beginnings

Both Bryce and I originally came from Western Australia. I was born in the country and grew up on a wheat and sheep farm and Bryce lived in Perth, in the suburbs. Our experiences of gardening were very different. In Perth to water the garden one turned on a tap and shifted sprinklers; in summer there were often water restrictions but it was still possible to have green lawns surrounding your house. On the farm all water for the house came from tanks; dam water was saved for the stock. We had a patch of scratchy buffalo grass no bigger than a carpet square. In Perth the soil is almost pure sand and easily tilled. The soil at the farm was heavy red clay, sticky in winter and rock hard in summer. To plant anything at all required a crowbar and a strong back. I remember my mother's excitement in planning a small rose bed. Ironically the beds had to be dug out, soil removed and sand added because all roses were budded on to Wichuraiana rootstock, which is only suitable for the sandy coastal soils of Perth. Two of those first roses that I remember were 'Picture', a warm pink with beautiful pointed buds and 'Peace', a gorgeous confection of cream, pink and yellow. For nostalgic reasons I have these two roses in my garden now.

'Peace', to my mother's generation, was a 'must have' rose, bred by Francis Meilland in France in the late 1930s. Fearing a German invasion he shipped cuttings of his beautiful rose to several growers around the world. The cuttings reached the USA on the last plane to leave France before the invasion, and in safety were propagated. The rose had several names before finally becoming known as 'Peace' in 1945. Because of its beauty – and because peace was so ardently desired and welcomed – it quickly became a best seller around the world. I bought mine, a climbing variety, after our eldest daughter returned from a posting with the RAAF to Qatar in 2003 for the allied invasion of Iraq.

My mother's garden expanded when what we called 'the scheme water' arrived. This was water which was originally pumped from Mundaring Weir, a dam in the Perth hills, to the Kalgoorlie Goldfields, a distance of 594km. At the time it was built – 1903 – this was hailed as a great feat of engineering. Much later, during the 1950s, feeder pipelines were distributed through the eastern wheat belt and we were the lucky winners when the pipeline went past our front boundary. Access to unlimited water made an enormous difference and more roses were planted. I remember a beautiful show of sweet peas growing over an old tin shed. In autumn the house was filled with armfuls of bronze chrysanthemums. I remember their pungent perfume to this day.

My mother must have been a very frustrated gardener in the early days as she had grown up in South Australia where her father had a beautiful garden. I say her father, because her mother surely would have not had time to spare for gardening: my mother was the eldest of nine children. We visited when I was about five and I remember a large circular lawn at the front of the house surrounded by roses and tall flowering things – probably hollyhocks. There was also a lovely glasshouse with a brick base and gable ends with a green door, in which grew begonias and ferns. In the backyard was a walnut tree big enough to climb, and further out an orchard. Grandfather also kept a cow, chooks and racing pigeons. Off the back veranda were steps leading down to a cellar, the first I had ever seen. My grandfather was a builder and constructed houses of Mount Gambier limestone with brick quoins, a style which seems peculiar to South Australia. His four sons all took up a trade and stayed in the family business. Perhaps this genetic background explains my interest in houses and gardens.

Reading has always played a big role in my life, and most of the books and magazines I was exposed to as a child were English. My mother subscribed to *The English Woman*, and for me, *Sunny Papers*. They were both full of pictures of quaint English cottages and gardens, in complete contrast to my harsh surroundings. I remember making 'fairy dells' under the shade of a passionfruit vine, feeling disappointed with the result and somehow realising that the fairy would have to be a pretty tough customer to survive there. Another clear memory I have is finding a patch of moss in the shade of a brick house we rented for a holiday in Perth. So lush, like green velvet, so perfect for fairies. When I was a little older my favourite book was *The Secret Garden*, and I was amazed to find that Mary also made fairy dells from flowers. I still read this book every now and then, and I am thrilled that my eldest granddaughter also loves it and shows signs of having caught the gardening bug.

ON THE BEACH

When Bryce and I married our first house was a small cottage 100 yards from the Indian Ocean, basically on a sand dune with a sea breeze, the 'Fremantle Doctor', which roared in at mid-morning every day. There was nothing growing on the block except some old gnarled tea trees and a few needle-sharp yuccas. About this time I had a book on growing bush gardens, which had been written with Sydney in mind. So we set out to grow a rainforest in the sand. We bought in loads of peatmoss, which must have come straight out of a swamp as we discovered a long-necked tortoise when we spread it round

the garden. We decided to build a pond for our tortoise in the front garden. We dug a small depression, lined it with black plastic and then drove up into the hills and helped ourselves to some lovely rocks and old tree logs to make our 'natural' pond. What with the peatmoss, the tortoise, and the removal of the rocks and logs, today it would be called an environmental tragedy. Despite the fact that most of the 'natives' we selected were totally unsuited to their environment, quite a lot grew, and by the time we left, five years later, we had made our first garden.

IN THE BUSH NEAR THE BEACH

Before too long we had two children and another due any day, and our little cottage was bursting at the seams. We were advised by a real estate agent to 'look at the land up the coast'. The block in question was in a small bushland development, about a kilometre from the sea, with a light covering of eucalypts and banksia. Dusk was falling, the crickets were singing, the bush smelled like Australian bush should smell and we decided to buy. That night, 23 December, child number three arrived and I spent Christmas in hospital doodling and designing our new home. The house we built among the trees was long and low, of red rustic brick and dark timber trim with clerestory windows to the north. At last we had our bush garden and, like a lot of 'native' devotees, not a single 'exotic' sullied our land.

This was when I also discovered French cooking and taught myself to cook through the monthly instalments of a magazine published by Cordon Bleu and the two volumes of *Mastering the Art of French Cooking* by Julia Child, L. Bertholle and Simone Beck. Month by month I cooked my way through French classic dishes. *The Classic Italian Cookbook* by Marcella Hazan introduced me to genuine Italian food and taught me how to balance a typical Italian meal. In later years I have turned to books by Patricia Wells, Maggie Beer, Stephanie Alexander and – last but not least – Jamie Oliver, who has made cooking fun and accessible to all. (Having mentioned just eight publications why is it that my shelves are overflowing with cookbooks?)

MOVING EAST

In 1979 we moved to Melbourne with three children, one dog, one cat and five goldfish in plastic boxes in tow. We were keen to build another house so looked at land. We felt that bush blocks were too far out for the children to travel on public transport to their schools

each day and decided to live closer in to the city. On an earlier 'looking at Melbourne' visit we had walked through the Botanical Gardens. It was the June long weekend and the elms were losing their leaves (deciduous trees were a novelty to us). The wet black asphalt paths were littered with fallen yellow heart-shaped leaves. It looked like the ground was studded with gold coins. Small black birds with orange accessories darted in and out of the shrubberies; so foreign to us, but also so familiar because of all those English books I had read. I decided there and then that I was going to love Melbourne.

As newcomers we tripped around getting to know our new state. Most weekends while we were living in rented accommodation we headed out sightseeing. We spent a lot of time in the Dandenongs, visiting great gardens such as Burnham Beeches, and also at Mount Macedon. On a smaller scale I also loved the kitchen garden at Heide, the museum of modern art on the banks of the Yarra river. We took a drive to Mount Baw Baw, hoping to see snow for the first time. There wasn't any snow but we did discover the most beautiful scenic drive along a ridge road between Noojee and the South Eastern Freeway. Small farms created a patchwork of greens and black-and-white cows dotted the paddocks like a toy farm set. Forested hills (to our eyes mountains, as we were accustomed to the flat farmland of Western Australia) made a backdrop to a stretch of water, the Tarago Reservoir – an idyllic setting. I thought to myself that I would love to live in this lovely green, lush, rural area one day.

THE GARDEN HOUSE

We built our first house in Melbourne, coincidentally called The Garden House, on a long skinny block (after we had demolished the existing modest 1930s house). The house was long and low with a lot of glass to the north, and had a wonderful kitchen. I began to dabble in catering. I took classes at the French Kitchen in Armadale and gave ambitious dinner parties. My heroine in the food world in Melbourne at that time was Mietta O'Donnell. To this day her restaurant (which was in Brunswick) is my ' best ever' in the city. I was also devouring the books of Elizabeth David (perhaps one of the most influential food writers of the twentieth century) and another lovely book, *The Taste of France*, which was full of beautiful photography of houses in regional France. This book whetted my appetite not only for the food but also for the traditional and appealing rural architecture of the farms and villages.

After the house was built the garden consisted of an out-of-control cypress hedge at the front and one golden plum and a large quince tree at the back. The latter delighted

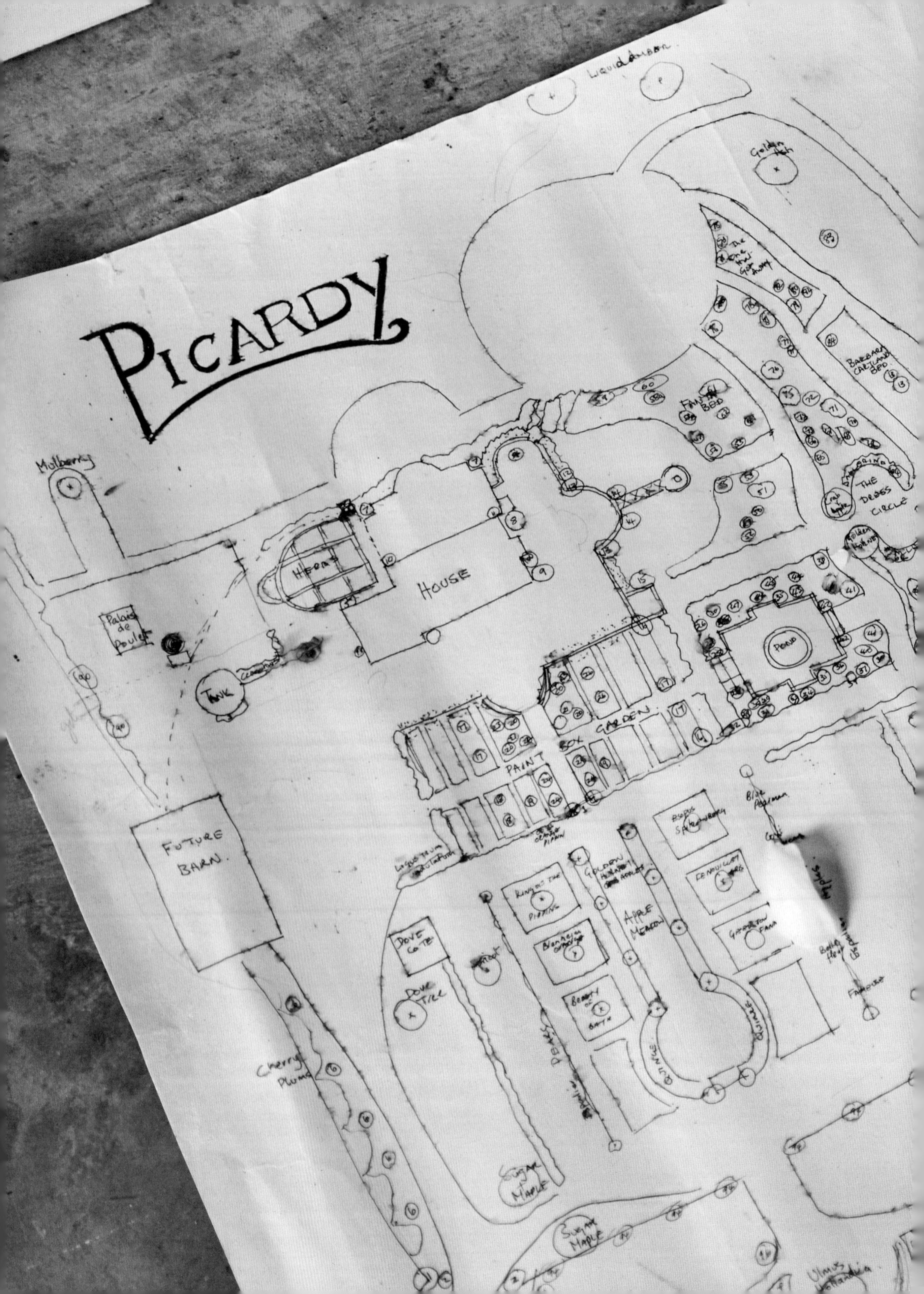
PICARDY
Liquidambar
Golden Ash
Mulberry
HERBS
HOUSE
Palais de Poule
TANK
FUTURE BARN
PAINT BOX GARDEN
POND
FAN BED
BARBARA CARTLAND BED
THE DRESS CIRCLE
APPLE MEADOW
King of the Pippins
Beauty of Bath
Blue Pearmain
DOVE COTE
Dove Tree
Pears
Quince
Cherry Plums
Sugar Maple
Sugar Maple
Ulmus Hollandica

us the first spring with its beautiful pale-pink single blossoms. The lawn was studded with Bellis perennis, English daisy and drifts of forget-me-nots, and a pretty bell-shaped white bulb filled the beds. Our new neighbour informed me that my pretty displays were weeds. The white bulb was particularly disliked. 'That's onion weed. You had better spray that.' It is all in the eye of the beholder.

I think of the garden that we made at this house as our transition garden. We planted a bit of a mixture of natives but also discovered silver birches, rhododendrons and camellias. Wisteria and ornamental grape thrived on our north-facing pergola. I was reading Vita Sackville-West and discovering that I wasn't the only one to think of having a white garden. I read about Edna Walling's gardens and her cottage housing development at Mooroolbark. I began a horticulture course at Burnley. I was garden mad, had run out of room and was captivated by the elegant old homes in Melbourne. So we moved again.

AN ARTS AND CRAFTS HOUSE

This time we moved further out of the city to the leafy suburbs and a solid two-storey Arts-and-Crafts-style house on a double block. The selling point was that there was room for a tennis court. That wasn't what I had in mind. The house had been owned by one family since it had been built in the early 1900s and needed redecorating throughout, and quite a bit of maintenance. The kitchen was very basic with a 1950s split-level gas stove sitting in a cream-tiled alcove where obviously an Aga slow-combustion stove had been. Out of interest I bought a copy of *The Trading Post*, the paper version of eBay, and it was meant to be: '4 oven Aga stove, $500'. With some difficulty it made its way to our house and looked as if it had always been there. I loved that stove.

Eventually, when we had finished painting, wallpapering and polishing boards inside the house, we turned to the garden. When we bought the house in winter an enormous silver birch in the centre of the garden was leafless, and by the beginning of summer it was still bare. A casualty of the drought we were experiencing, or perhaps just old age. There were some big rhododendrons, an overgrown shrubbery, a golden ash, lots of self-sown euphorbia and a large bed of cacti of all shapes and sizes, which I removed. I have always felt a bit guilty about this, because although I loathe cacti some of them may have been rare.

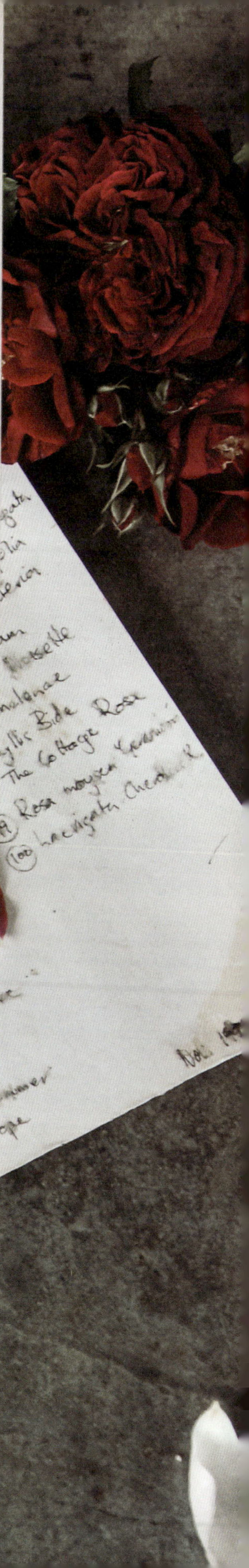

Bryce and I found this old garden hard to put our stamp on. The soil was riddled with tree roots and new plants didn't seem to thrive. Two of our children moved out of home (one to reappear at odd intervals for some years!) and our much-loved dog, Polly, escaped on garbage collection day and was run over on the busy road which was also proving to be very noisy. We began to think of downsizing to a small city house and pursuing the dream – a weekend place in the country.

A LITTLE PINK BIJOUX

We bought a pretty little derelict Edwardian bijoux weatherboard house in original condition. It must have been the smallest rooming house in Melbourne. There were three little kitchens, one inside and two others in various sheds in the tiny back yard. We removed layer upon layer of carpet and lino until we came to the 1910 newspaper and lovely Baltic pine boards. Another reno job and we had a pretty little pale-pink house. The garden was miniscule which was just what we wanted, because now we were seriously thinking of the country weekender.

2

Finding our land

We had been spending a lot of time with friends at their farm at Castlemaine, an old goldmining town, and liked the history, the stone buildings and the culture there, but as the main desire was to have a garden we felt the summer climate was too difficult for weekenders. We decided to revisit the West Gippsland area that had so impressed us in the first weeks of our arrival in Victoria. Once more the greenness, the lushness and the softness of the landscape captured our interest. We seriously began our search for land.

Our wish list read: 'Vacant land with a building permit – Not too big – 10–12 acres – Some mature trees – European trees preferably'. We looked at many properties. One property had a vertiginous drive which hair-pinned itself up a very steep hill then levelled off briefly before plunging into a thickly forested ravine on the other side. At another the trees grew parallel to the ground, forced into unnatural positions by gale-force prevailing winds.

One golden late spring afternoon we found our spot, described in real-estate jargon as 'Twenty-four acres of vacant farming land with red/chocolate soil, a good rainfall, 40 inch av., a spring-fed willow-lined creek, picturesque rural views', and most importantly, 'with a building permit'. Although quite a few of the items on our wish list were missing – no significant trees – more land than we wanted (we saw ourselves as gardeners, not farmers), the borrowed landscape of green rolling hills with stands of cypress trees that gave a 'European' feel seemed to speak to us and we felt we could make this little private valley our home. The agent assured us that we would have 'no troubles' leasing any excess land to local farmers and that 'trees grow like stink round here'. On both accounts he has been proved right. We had found our blank canvas.

GETTING TO KNOW THE LAND

During the period before construction of the house began, we often visited the property. The creek was overrun with blackberries scrambling 20 feet in the air in a thorny impenetrable jungle. We hacked them off at the bottom and then pulled and dragged them into the paddock to be burned at a later date. It was a painful but satisfying process

to expose the narrow willow-lined creek. In all the years we have been here, this little creek which oozes out of the side of the hill in our neighbours' paddock and meanders in and out of our boundaries has never dried up, even in times of drought, and the volume of water appears to be constant in all seasons. It became evident just how much water flows when a culvert became blocked, and in a matter of days a lake formed in the valley. Even more surprising was how quickly the water birds discovered this new haven. Unfortunately the lake was not on our property and the farmer, not keen on seeing his land disappear under water, unblocked the culvert and the creek continued on its merry way, ultimately ending in the reservoir.

On hot summer evenings we would drive from Melbourne with friends or family for picnics. While it was still light we would tramp through the creek area exploring, in our naivety never giving a thought to snakes. On one occasion our dog, Molly, ran ahead of us over what I thought was a piece of black plastic pipe which suddenly slithered off the path. A wake-up call – even in paradise there are serpents.

As the darkness fell we lay on our backs in the grass, smelling that wonderful scent of freshly mown hay and gazing at the emerging stars. The open expanse of sky was to become as important to us as the landscape. By day passing clouds created an ever-changing panorama, and by night the Milky Way was like a diamond bracelet in the sky. One evening we watched the full moon rise over the hill, the huge pale-golden disk seeming to hover on the horizon and looking just like a child's drawing of the Man in the Moon with his smiling face. Satellite-watching competitions also entertained us. It was amazing to realise how many tracked across the night sky.

It was an exciting time on the verge of a wonderful new project.

SITING THE HOUSE

The first decision to be made was where in the 24 acres should we site the house. The previous owners had planned to build quite close to the road on the western boundary, and almost directly opposite another house. In this position there was a glimpse of the Tarago Reservoir. This didn't appeal to us, so we sought and received permission to build on the lower portion of the land and enter from the road on our southern boundary. We were fortunate that a large roadside eucalypt had died just where we wished to put our entrance (we may not have got permission to remove a living tree). From this site we had a view to the north up the valley in which the creek ran. The hills around us formed a protective basin. No other dwellings were in sight – just a few old sheds. We could see the horizon where the sky met the green paddocks all around us. It felt safe and secluded.

THE DESIGN PROCESS

The next decision to be made was the design and the look of the house.

I knew I wanted to create a French-style farmhouse, but every region in France has its own architecture. The lush green landscape suggested mid to northern France rather than the south.

We decided to call the property 'Picardy', this being our first landfall in France, and also because of the old song 'Roses are blooming in Picardy'; the intention was to have a garden overflowing with roses. Researching French vernacular buildings, I discovered that a typical Picardian farmhouse has high gable ends, so the shape of the house was decided. Because the house was to be a weekender we wanted it to be very simple and small. I designed a rectangular living space with two brick chimneys at either end, divided by a staircase leading to two upstairs bedrooms. A single-storey section held a mudroom for boots and coats, a store cupboard, laundry and bathroom.

To me the details that give a house that French feel are the symmetry of the doors and windows. The windows have to be made of timber, casement style, the correct proportions and open inwards; and of course, the doors have to be French! Even in much grander old French houses it was common for houses to be only one room deep, which creates a light and airy feel, and for the rooms to be linked together without corridors. With the openings aligned this creates what the French call an *enfilade*. This works well in public rooms but is perhaps not so desirable in the bedrooms. In our modest farmhouse we have a double enfilade from the kitchen to the sitting room and out the French doors to the garden. In 2017 this feature was extended when we added another room to the house.

Perhaps the most obvious items that say 'French style' are shutters. These were part of the original design but unfortunately are still on the drawing board, and Maison Picardy is still waiting for that final touch. Perhaps, twenty-five years later they may soon eventuate.

PICARDY
420

CHOOSING THE MATERIAL

We had to decide what material to build the house in. We considered using concrete blocks with a render to emulate the traditional *crépis* plaster finish used in some regions of France. We had often visited Montsalvat at Eltham, a group of cottages, studios, workshops, a great hall and wonderful farm buildings, which had been set up as an artists' colony in the late 1930s. An eclectic mix of materials has been used there, but it all seems to blend into a harmonious whole. One of the cottages at Montsalvat is built of rammed earth – or more prettily in French, *pise de terre*. The thickness of 30-centimetre-rammed-earth walls and the method of building suited the symmetrical style of the house that I had designed. The deal was sealed when we met Rick, a charming man, who is now known affectionately to our family as 'Rick the rammer'.

The earth for the walls, usually used for road sand, was sourced from a quarry nearby. When the first load was delivered to the site I was beside myself with excitement. The colour was deep terracotta. All the rammed earth buildings I had seen in Victoria previously had been a greyish colour, the colour of the raw material. We had considered that we would limewash the building a soft apricot-pink, but this would not be necessary. Au naturelle, our walls would be the perfect colour.

3 The rammed earth house

On 1 August 1993 the building began with a bulldozer cutting a curving driveway through the paddock to the site of the proposed house. As the sun rose over the hill, the chocolate soil was exposed for the first time – it looked and smelt good enough to eat.

I became a bit of a builders' groupie hanging around the site and not wanting to miss a thing. While I was occupied 'supervising', Bryce was busy working in Melbourne making it all possible. I watched the footings being dug, the concrete slab being poured and was there most days once the ramming of the walls began. The earth for the walls was mixed with white cement – which acts as a stabiliser – by a Bobcat. The mix was then dumped into formwork to a depth of 30 centimetres. The action of ramming then compressed the soil by two thirds. Basically it is a method of producing artificial stone, a process which in nature takes thousands of years. Layer by layer the apricot-coloured walls rose quite quickly. The end gable walls were completed first and from a distance looked like an ancient ruined abbey abandoned in a forgotten valley.

The ramming crew camped on site, the two boys sleeping in their cars and the boss, Rick, sleeping on the tray of his ute, partially covered by a tarpaulin. A pile of chimney bricks and a briefcase served as the site office. It was August with typical equinox weather – some days sunny and pleasant and others cold with wild winds. A Sunday picnic was planned to celebrate the birthday of one of the crew. It was an absolutely freezing day with a gale-force wind blowing straight through the glassless windows and the gaps where the brick chimneys were to go. The gourmet picnic lunch was set out on a makeshift table in what was to be the sitting room. With the wind whistling and whipping our hair, we ploughed stoically through our lunch, having a lot of fun and laughs despite the appalling conditions.

One weekend we decided to camp overnight on site with the crew (the ramming crew worked seven days a week). I cooked a pot roast with all the trimmings in a camp oven and we lingered around the campfire drinking red wine long into the night. Eventually Bryce and I staggered off in the dark to our two-man tent. This was quite an adventure for me as I have never been keen on roughing it. During the night it began to rain and as an under-canvas-ignoramus I touched the roof, which promptly began to drip on my side of the tent. A long night, and an experience which has not been repeated!

This method of construction – ramming – is very, very noisy. The pneumatic rammer is driven by a compressor which creates its own noise, and added to this din is the constant 'thwack' as the soil is compressed inside the formwork. Positioned as we are, enclosed by hills, echoes reverberated around the surrounding country. Although we were hidden away in a valley it was no secret that something peculiar was happening. Curious people turned up and had a turn with 'Big Foot", the pneumatic rammer.

Some of our visitors were sceptical about the method of construction and the strength of the 'dirt' walls. 'Just wait till the wombats get stuck into those walls. They'll love it!' one doubtful Thomas commented to Rick. 'Yeah,' answered Rick seriously with a deadpan face, 'they do love it, but they have a bit of trouble with the bank manager.' It took a while for our sceptic to realise that Rick was taking the mickey.

Most building sites I am sure have a drama where something goes wrong. Ours occurred on a Monday morning. The previous day's walls were revealed when the formwork was removed. Quelle horreur! A top-floor window at the front of the house was not correctly aligned. The decision was made that the top part of the wall had to be brought down. The wall was scored with a deep cut above the downstairs window to encourage a clean break. Rick raised the bucket of the Bobcat and pushed from inside the house. The rest of us stood back safely out of way. As the wall fell the bobcat reared up like a bucking bronco and teetered on its rear wheels as if to fall backwards. Everyone held their breath– except me. I screamed out an obscenity that sounded remarkably like a passing crow (and I never quite regained my dignity as they constantly reminded me of my lapse in decorum over the following weeks). Fortunately the Bobcat landed safely with its four wheels on the ground and (waste not, want not) the broken pieces of wall I later used to build steps and a retaining rockery in the garden.

After three weeks and the departure of the earth wall team the conventional build began. The next item on the agenda was the roof. Unfortunately a traditional French-style roof of stone or slate was out of the question. Flat schist stone doesn't exist in Victoria and slate was too expensive. The local terracotta tiles lacked that handmade artisan look so we chose galvanised iron, a traditional material used both in Australia and in France for humble farm buildings.

We did choose terracotta tiles for the floors. These came from China, were very thick and definitely handmade. Several of them are inscribed with Chinese script (I like to imagine they are lunch orders) and some have little animal and bird footprints.

THE ROOMS

We envisioned living a simple life in our *petite maison*, cooking and eating in the same space – a traditional country kitchen. I had never quite got over leaving behind my beautiful old Aga when we had last moved house and I decided to look for a woodburning stove. Once again I consulted *The Trading Post* and an advertisement for a Canadian stove caught my eye. We travelled to Cockatoo and found the stove outside on the back veranda. She was a black-and-cream enamel, chrome-trimmed beauty from Elmira, Ontario. On the firebox door was written her name in red: 'Sweetheart'. She had a bread-proving-cum-warming drawer at the top, a cast-iron cook top, a deep oven and sat on stumpy little chrome cabriole legs which were engraved with hearts. Sweetheart was straight out of *The Little Golden Books* of my childhood. How could I resist! I had no idea how old she was or how she found her way to Australia, but she is still cooking up a storm for us twenty-five years later.

Under the window we had a white tile-topped bench built with open shelves with wicker baskets underneath, copied from a picture of a French kitchen. An old wooden office desk became a workbench and a row of cupboards with chicken-wire inserts held crockery, glasses and foodstuffs. The chicken wire caused a visiting farmer to comment laconically, 'Gawd! The blowflies are pretty bad around here, but they're are not THAT big!'

Recently we have updated the kitchen, replacing the open shelves with deep drawers, and adding a dishwasher.

THE SITTING ROOM

A staircase divides the kitchen from the sitting room. The simple iron balustrading and bannisters were made by Rick, wearing his blacksmith's hat. The heart of a country home to me is an open fireplace, and either side of this now sit a pair of 1930s club chairs. My grandparents gave these chairs and a matching box couch to my parents as a wedding present, and when the latter died I inherited them. They have been re-covered numerous times over the years and I have been sitting in them on and off my whole life. For their new home (my first attempt at upholstery) I covered my mother's floral Sanderson linen with gingham loose covers. I was too nervous to spend much on fabric in case I mucked it up so I bought a whole roll of blue-and-white gingham which cost me $1.79 a metre. With the equivalent of an *Upholstery for Dummies* book by my side I launched into the

project. I was very pleased with the result. They are now ready for their third makeover in this house and I am considering using painter's drop cloth fabric (only this time I won't be making them!).

THE BEDROOMS

The upper floor is divided by a small landing, which has a window to give a bird's-eye view of the parterre-style garden which was planned for the front of the house. To the left is the main bedroom, which for years was Spartan in decoration and comfort. In the early years we were too busy in the garden for afternoon naps and fell into bed at night exhausted, so the aesthetics of our surroundings didn't really matter. Gradually I have collected bibs and bobs to furnish this room. My favourite pieces are the two armoires, which were a nasty stained redwood when I bought them at auction. They are much prettier now I have painted them a soft grey.

The dormitory, on the right side of the landing, is furnished with a pretty 1930s Tasmanian oak wardrobe and old black cast-iron beds. One of them was Bryce's mother's bed when she was a small girl. Lined up along the wall they resemble a scene from the Madeline books set in a Paris convent.

MOVING IN

It was a rainy Christmas Eve when we finally moved in. The family arrived in dribs and drabs to celebrate our first Christmas in the country. What a relief to find on Christmas morning that Santa had found the right chimney! I was up bright and very early to light Sweetheart for the first time. I was a little apprehensive as the maiden cook was to be the Christmas turkey. I soon had a roaring fire going and the turkey in the oven. I could have slept in a little later – the little red button to tell me when it was cooked popped up at 10.30 a.m.!

It was a very special Christmas Day for us in our brand-new farmhouse.

Boxing Day found us marooned in a sea of red mud. The weather was wintery. We lit the fires and hunkered down, waiting for the rain to stop and the mud to dry up.

Early in January we began to turn our minds to painting the doors and windows. We had guests staying with us who professed to like painting. Serendipity! In my mind's eye I could see the perfect washed-out French blue. Bryce was very patient as my collection of sample pots grew. Eventually a decision was made and the painting began, but I am still searching for that elusive perfect milky-blue.

ABCDEFGHI
IKLMNOPQR
STUVWXYZ
abcdefghijklmno
pqrstuvwxyz

Sweet Heart

4

Shaping the garden

With the house now finished our thoughts turned to the garden.

THE GRAVEL FORECOURT AND PAINTBOX PICKING BEDS

Our ideas for the size of the garden at this time were quite unambitious. After all, we were weekenders only. The first thing I did was to design a gravelled entrance forecourt at the front of the house. I decided on gravel because it is traditionally used in France, and is the perfect surface for playing the game of *pétanque or boules*. (Guess who had received a set for Christmas that year?) Also I was now aware of the possibility of snakes in our garden of Eden and I wanted a bare space in front of the house.

The semi-circular shape of the gravel and the paintbox beds were inspired by Monet's garden at Giverny, which we had visited many years before. The parterre-type shapes were chosen because, like Giverny, the garden is overlooked by the upstairs bedrooms. We decided to divide the beds with brick weeder paths and to quarter the whole space with gravel paths. We mapped out the shapes with string and each weekend during autumn and winter Bryce laid the brick paths. As the beds were formed I trundled out to the paddocks with the wheelbarrow, gathering cow manure to enrich the soil. Our first plan was to have a picking garden overflowing with roses, flowers, herbs and vegetables. The first year the growth in the virgin soil was prodigious. Beans towered overhead as though sown by Jack from the magical beanstalk story, and beautiful Shirley poppies filled the beds with tissue-paper flowers subtly striped in pinks, reds, white and grey. To semi-enclose this area we planted cuttings of *Lavandula dentata* in front of the house and *Ligustrum undulatum* to separate the parking area from the garden. In time they grew into a hedge.

I had always admired in pictures of European gardens the use of espaliered apples as garden fences or dividers. Using the advice given in an old 1930s gardening book we chose bare-rooted apple whips, small trees without lateral branches, and planted them the first winter at the back of the paintbox beds against a fence of two single wires 300 millimetres apart. It took an act of faith to cut the whips off at the height of the bottom

wire, leaving three buds, one to grow vertically and the others to become the 'arms'. Our book instructed us to let them grow 300 millimetres then pinch out the growing tips of the laterals and to allow the vertical shoot to grow past the top wire and then pinch out the tip, leaving two buds to form the top lateral. It sounds complicated but when the plant is before you it makes sense. To our astonishment it worked! Within the first year our little espaliers had reached the top wire and were growing strongly. Making this apple fence has been one of the most satisfying aspects of our garden, and we have repeated it in other areas with both apples and pears. A mistake we made was to choose apples on normal rootstocks, as at the time we were unaware of dwarf rootstock. This has meant that with age they have grown very vigorously and send up tall summer shoots, which Bryce now hedges.

Our initial vision of this garden is now reality, although the vegetables have moved to their own space and the lavender hedge has been replaced with blue-and-white plumbago. This has not quite worked out as I imagined. The plumbago doesn't like our cold winters and the leaves turn a sickly yellow, but in summer it grows rampantly and to keep it at the required height we have to clip regularly. This means that we are constantly cutting off the flower buds and my vision of a summer blue-and-white border remains a vision.

The star roses in this garden are the shrub rose 'Gruss an Aachen' – a delicious creamy, pink-to-apricot many-petalled rose with gorgeous perfume which flowers singly and in clusters – and 'Sylvia', a florist's long-stemmed hybrid tea rose, dark pink and chosen because it shares my late mother's name.

In standard version –which in retrospect I would not choose again as wind is always a problem and I find stakes ugly – are 'Souvenir de St Anne's', pale blush-pink with loose-petalled flowers; 'Charles de Gaulle', pinky-mauve with large typical hybrid tea pointed buds and flowers; and last but not least the ubiquitous 'Iceberg'. Poor 'Iceberg': a rose that performs so well that it is seen in some circles as 'common'. But if it was good enough for Vita Sackville-West's white garden it is good enough for me. It is generous, disease-free, has lovely foliage, continuously repeats and makes a great cut flower. What's not to like? Fashion in plants is a funny thing. I once attended a garden lecture in Melbourne and the speaker was Beth Chatto, the eminent plantswoman from England. She had visited the Dandenongs that day and commented on 'the beautiful red-tipped hedges of photinia'. A groan of dislike came from the audience, and she received a similar response when she showed a slide of wild fennel growing in Italy.

In spring the paintbox beds are now crammed with the roses in bloom; Californian poppies in shades of creamy pink, lemon and a rogue, rather bright, enamel orange; tall spires of pink, mauve and white foxgloves; dainty fern-leafed aquilegia with pretty pastel old-fashioned flowering bonnets; clumps of pink and white species gladioli and sweet peas romp over all. The perfume is intoxicating.

In summer and into autumn roses and Californian poppies continue and are joined by mauve and white cosmos 'Sensation', crisp white and yellow-centred shasta daisies, cream salvias, white and mauve dahlias, tall purple *Verbena bonariensis*, artemesias with flat umbels of pastel flowers and waving fronds of pink-and-white *Gaura lindheimeri*. It is easy to see where the common name 'Dancing Butterflies' comes from. All year round violets and erigeron embroider the edges.

This riot of plants has now become self-perpetuating and self-sows each season. I have a *laissez-faire* attitude to weeds. If they are pretty – buttercups, lawn daisy or wild oats and grasses from stable manure – and add to the general effect I am trying to achieve, they are safe. The only weeds I abhor are sticky weed, spurge, sorrel, milk thistles and, the worst of all, blackberry.

THE HERB GARDEN

When the structure of the paintbox beds was complete, with some leftover bricks I made a herb garden on the north side of the house. This was quite a complicated design and I surprised myself to find that not only had my mathematical calculations worked out but also that I could lay bricks! I filled the beds with culinary herbs and I love having them a step away from the kitchen. Each Christmas I make large *bouquets garnis* of lemon thyme, sage, savory and marjoram for the Christmas turkey and big bunches of bay leaves, to keep away the pantry moths, as small gifts for friends.

Full of confidence after my bricklaying efforts I moved on to a crazy-paved path made from leftover offcuts of the terracotta floor tiles. Sometimes it was easier to use up 'leftovers' as it was too hard to dispose of them. I took advice from the late Margot Knox, a doyenne of mud bricks and paving. Her advice to me was, 'always use the biggest and best pieces closest to the house'. Despite being laid straight on to the ground with no cement at all this path has stood the test of time.

THE CRAB APPLE WALK AND HERITAGE APPLE AND PEAR ORCHARD

In a direct line with the front door, and to create an axis from the paintbox garden, we planted an avenue of 'Golden Hornet' crab apples. We borrowed this idea after a visit to the now late Joan Law-Smith's garden at Bolobek, Macedon, a wonderful and inspirational garden. She had finished her avenue with a circle of box hedge backed with rhododendrons. A beautiful marble statue of a young girl on a stone plinth created a focal point. We chose to make a circle of quinces and left the circle open as we planned to continue the axis to a nuttery in the future.

On either side of the avenue of crab apples we planted six varieties of heritage apple trees and, continuing the French theme, chose varieties with names such as 'Brabant Belle Fleur' and 'Fenouillet Gris', planted in a grid pattern. At first we mowed paths, leaving squares of longer grass around the trees to create a checkerboard effect. As the trees matured and bore fruit this became impractical and they are now underplanted with white violets, white daffodils, pink sparaxis, blue ipheion and pink and white Japanese wind anemones. To enclose this orchard we espaliered one side with four apple trees – 'Fameuse', 'Esopus Spitzenburg', 'Belle de Boskoop' and 'Cox's Orange Pippin' – and the other with four pears, two 'Beurre Bosc' and two 'Sensation'. The pears are not nearly as prolific as the apples. My favourite is 'Beurre Bosc', a beautiful firm cooking pear.

Now in spring this area is a fairyland, buzzing with bees in the pink and white blossom. When the apples ripen in autumn the trees are alive with parrots scoffing the fruit. We still have more than we can consume – there is a limit to how many apple crumbles and tarte tatins two people can eat! Cider making has been discussed as a possibility.

To mark the entrance to the crab apple walk I wished to have a simple structure to support a climbing rose. I wanted to use bush poles for a rustic effect, *à la* Jardins du Prieuré Nôtre-Dame d'Orsan (a garden in the Berry region of France, which I unfortunately have only visited vicariously through books). Being impatient I set out alone to visit a small sawmill out in the middle of the bush. I arrived at 'smoko' time. As I walked towards a circle of blokes looking like they had come from central casting for the film *Deliverance* I began to think that it wasn't a very smart idea. I stuttered out what I was looking for and showed them some pictures. No, bush poles weren't their thing, but one guy – 'Bull' – with arms like hams and a grizzled ginger forelock and beard said he might be able to help me. Feeling foolish (and wishing I was anywhere but a sawmill in the middle of the bush) I gave him the address. 'I'll drop 'em off after work,' he said. That afternoon I waited. No sign of Bull. Eventually, at about 10.30 p.m., I decided that the delivery was not to take place, and went to bed. But then my blood ran cold as the lights of a vehicle came up the drive. I double-granny-knotted my dressing gown and, feeling very vulnerable, went downstairs. 'Who is it?' I squeaked. 'It's me, Bull, I've got youse's poles.' I peeked out and there was a 4WD and inside were four kids in their pyjamas. Apparently Bull couldn't deliver during daylight hours as he was *sans* licence, didn't have a trailer so he had dragged the poles behind the 4WD, and had the kids because the wife was working. One of the twins needed its nappy changed and we all ended up in the kitchen having a high old time. Periodically after that Bull and his wife and family dropped in to see how we were getting on. The wife thought we were mad living 'stuck out here ... don't you get scared at night by yourself?'

Now I had my bush poles I convinced our son and a couple of his friends to build our first structure, a rustic arch. At first it looked rather like a gallows, but with the addition of some rough lattice work and the rambler roses 'Albertine' and 'New Dawn' it quickly became a bower of beauty. Unfortunately Bull's bush poles, which I suspect came from a roadside verge, didn't last very long and were replaced with treated pine poles. Not as nice, but a lot less stressful.

THE SHORT WALK AND THE POND ROSE GARDEN

To the east the land sloped gently away from the gravel forecourt. The natural lay of the land suggested a wide path leading out to future developments. To change levels we made a broad brick-edged step filled with gravel. A visiting neighbour remarked that it reminded him of a grave top. Ignoring this we pushed on and pegged out our new path. We decided to make this a wide grass path with an herbaceous border on either side. I chose a pastel colour scheme of pinks, blues and mauves with grey foliage. Very pretty, very English Home Counties. Of course it wasn't too long before a few roses snuck in to make a mixed border, and now they tend to dominate.

The path and the paintbox garden now formed an L-shape and made a space for another garden. We were about to celebrate an important wedding anniversary, and on spotting a cement cattle trough at a farming field day it occurred to us that it was the perfect proportions for a pond for this space and would make a lovely reflective pool. I envisaged a sunken pool, and as this was beyond our capabilities we organised a man with a digger to come to excavate a hole. This was a luxury as up until now all earthworks

had been done with spade, rake, wheelbarrow and hard work. The 3.6-metre diameter trough was delivered and craned into the hole and hey presto! a pond. Pink water lilies were added to provide shelter for fish and tadpoles. Repeating the theme of the paintbox garden we edged the pond and garden with bricks to marry the two formal areas together.

My love affair with old-fashioned roses now took off. A local nursery put out a wonderful rose catalogue and this and other publications such as rose books by Susan Irvine and Peter Beale became my bedtime reading. I drooled over the descriptions and finally chose a selection of roses mostly with French names: 'Duchesse de Brabant', a soft pink, muddle-petalled rose that repeats continuously; 'Honorine de Brabant', a pink-and-white-striped rose; 'Fantin Latour', with clusters of sugar-pink cup-shaped blooms, spring flowering only, generous and very beautiful. A later addition has been the French-bred Delbard rose 'Monet', with large pink-and-white candy-stripe blooms. Growing on an arbour are 'Madame Alfred Carrière', a pale-whisper-pink climber – and everybody's favourite, the pink-and-white 'Pierre de Ronsard'. The pond rose garden was soon full, and I cast my eye around for another spot to indulge my passion.

THE HORSESHOE BEDS

At the east end of the house two pairs of French doors either side of the fireplace opened on to the garden. We decided to continue the gravel and brick edging and repeat the shape we had used at the front of the house. The soil in this area was poor as the topsoil had been lost when excavations for plumbing had taken place. What remained was heavy clay suitable for making bricks. The first year I scattered a packet of meadow mix – Flanders poppies and cornflowers – and with the weeds – hawkbit, dandelion and fog grass – miraculously a very pretty sward of meadow grew. This was not a permanent solution, however, because for months of the year it was either a sticky muddy mess or a dust bowl. We decided to edge the brick semi-circle with a garden bed, have an open area of grass and then make a large horseshoe-shaped bed for more roses. Because of the quality of the soil I decided to double dig the beds and incorporate organic matter and manure. Getting the manure was not a problem. The cows left a continuous supply; just a quick duck under the electric hot-wire fence and out into the paddock with my trusty iron-wheeled barrow. Double digging was another matter. I don't think I have ever been so thin, fit or exhausted since.

We broke up the horseshoe-shaped bed in the middle with an iron arbour, which we had made locally from reinforcement rods, and planted either side the gorgeous cupped-and-quartered pale-pink climbing rose 'Souvenir de Malmaison'. Crammed inside her medium-sized buds are a multitude of petals, which in wet weather can become a ball of mould. She is like the little girl in the nursery rhyme: 'When she is good she is very, very good, but when she is bad she is horrid.' Planted to intertwine with the Souvenirs is pale-pink *Clematis montana*, and at her feet are clumps of the pale-pink trumpet-flowered crinum lily.

For the north side of the bed I chose cream- and apricot-coloured roses including 'Perle d'Or, a pale-coral-pink rose with tiny perfect buds; 'Perdita', a creamy David Austin; 'Abraham Darby', a large shrub rose with outer pale-pink ripple-edged petals and an apricot centre; 'Buff Beauty', a spreading rose and with generous flowers exactly as named; and 'Devoniensis', sometimes known as the Magnolia rose, opening to a flat dish of rich cream. In this bed also is 'Heidesomme', with lovely clusters of creamy-white small ruffled flowers opening from soft lemon buds. The strong perfume from this rose is quite unusual – almost a fresh citrus. *Euphorbia wulfenii*, with its glaucous foliage and brought from a previous garden, now spreads all through this bed.

The southern and pink bed has 'Cecile Brunner', the Sweetheart rose, with soft-pink baby buds opening to muddled rosettes; 'Reine Victoria', a lanky shrub, with sugar-pink goblets; and Rosa centifolia, pink-and-white-striped, also known as the Village Maid, which remind me of old-fashioned little girls' pinafores. *Rosa roxburghi*, known as the Chestnut rose because of its prickly hips, has pale-pinky-mauve outer petals and a darker centre. *Rosa glauca*, chosen for the dusty burgundy foliage, has small single magenta blooms and interesting black hips. Intermingling with the pink roses is a bush of pink rosemary and foxgloves in spring, and in late summer perennial asters. If I can find a space I like to scatter seeds of cosmos and cornflowers.

THE VINE TERRACE

The last area to complete the circumnavigation of the house was the terrace at the back. Three sets of French doors opened on to this north-facing aspect. We chose to keep this side very simple, with brick paving to link the herb garden and the crazy-paved path to the gravel on the east side. Bryce was going overseas on business so before he left he levelled the area and my project was to lay the bricks before he returned. Two weeks later

I picked him up from the airport and drove back to Picardy where we opened a bottle of French champagne to celebrate his homecoming and my completion of the vine terrace.

I had collected some old cast-iron, grape-clustered light brackets and from these we had made a support for an ornamental grapevine to shade the house and the new brick terrace.

THE DOVECOTE

A friend commented one day, 'What this garden needs is a folly.' I am sure that a lot of people might think that a *faux* French house in Gippsland would already qualify as a folly, but we took the suggestion on board. I had always been charmed by the *pigeonniers* or *colombiers* (depending in what area of France they come from) – dovecotes in English. Traditionally in French rural areas they were an important part of farm buildings. Pigeons provided food and fertiliser, bred very easily and required a very small space. We were already thinking of adding further accommodation as boy- and girlfriends became part of the family. Perhaps we could build a mud-brick dovecote in preparation for tackling a barn?

We read up all the books and manuals and 'nuts-and-berries' type publications to learn all we could about mud-brick construction. Very soon it was obvious that we would need two lifetimes if we were to make the bricks ourselves. We sourced a supplier of mud bricks and approached a timber yard to order the posts that would form the corners of the dovecote. 'What ya building?!' expostulated the timberman when I told him I wanted four massive posts 300 x 300 millimetres square and 5 metres in length. When I told him it was for a 6 x 6 foot building he looked at me as if I was crazy. I guess that is the whole point of a folly.

The building began with the delivery of the concrete for the miniscule slab. Whoops! A slight miscalculation with the quantity needed. The overflow was shovelled into buckets and any container we could lay our hands on. Weekend after weekend the family toiled away as the walls slowly rose. My daughter and I laid bricks, Bryce mixed the mortar by hand in a barrow and our son kept up the brick supply to the bricklayers. The *pièce de résistance* was the square pitched roof, which our future son-in-law was in charge of. Six months later we finished the dovecote. It was a unanimous decision that we would not be building a barn ourselves.

TIME OUT

While all this planning, planting and construction were taking place we were at the same time becoming acquainted with our neighbours and our little town. When initially searching for land I had not given much thought to the importance of the proximity of a town. After all we were Melbourne-based and only staying at the property at weekends and bringing all our requirements with us. What a pleasure to discover the convenience of our town, only a 4-kilometre drive away, that had everything you could possibly need.

A great little supermarket provided good fruit and vegetables. In the early days Saturday morning at the supermarket was a social occasion. If you spent over $25 a tombola was spun and you received a prize. We met many new people in the queue while Saturday shopping. The friendly family-run butcher's shop sold fantastic local meat and there were two cheese factories within striking distance. Added to these businesses were a hotel, two garages, hairdresser, woodfired bakery, grainstore, hardware, newsagent, post office, pharmacy, milk bar, veterinary clinic, two churches, two schools, police station, doctor's rooms and a hospital. Not bad for somewhere that the sign at the edge of town said had 500 residents.

Fortunately over the years we have not required the services of the hospital, but indirectly it has provided us with a lot of entertainment. Fundraising has been the excuse for many a good shindig.

We have attended a three-course dinner in a marquee in a private garden, catered for by the ladies of the Hospital Auxillary, with a local combo playing cool jazz. The next year the theme was tweaked and we attended 'Jazz After Dark' in the local hall. To gain entrance we had to creep around the back of the hall and into a barely lit space decorated as a speakeasy, with painted backdrops of the Chicago night skyline. This time the music was more upbeat and we swung to some hot jazz.

'Christmas in July' was held in the football pavilion, which was magically transformed with 2-metre-tall 'Christmas tree' cones dotted between the round damask-covered candlelit tables. The trees were completely covered with white Christmas lilies, glasshouse-grown locally. The perfume was breathtaking. Christmas dinner was served, with all the trimmings.

In December, the 'proper' month for Christmas, 'Carols by Candlelight' is held on the football oval, beginning at dusk with a picnic on the grass. As well as the traditional sing-along of well-known carols, talented members of the community perform on a

makeshift platform (the back of a large truck). The finale takes place when darkness falls. With all lights flashing, the fire brigade enters carrying Santa Claus, who distributes lollies to the pack of excited children swarming around him.

Their most ambitious function we have attended was 'A Confederate Ball at Tara'. We arrived, appropriately costumed – 'Scarlett' in the picnic-scene dress and 'Rhett' in grey tails – parked in a paddock and were driven by horse and coach to the gates of 'Tara', the property. There was a mizzle of rain and darkness was falling, and before us out of the gloom appeared an encampment of Confederate soldiers. Outside small tents, fires smoked, over which pots hung on tripods. Soldiers, dressed in their grey uniforms, quietly went about their business preparing dixies of food and tending to their tethered horses. Horses snuffled in their nosebags, while others stamped and harness jangled. It was one of the most surreal events that I have ever experienced. The evening continued with dinner and dancing in a large barn, with conventional loud modern music. In such a setting we should have been dancing a cotillion to the sound of a fiddle. At the end of the evening we were conveyed by horse and coach to our car and back to the twentieth century. We learnt later that our 'soldiers' were a group of men, keen horsemen, who had a special interest in the Confederate cavalry of the American Civil War. They had a hierarchy of rank and took the whole thing very seriously.

The local Landcare group and The Country Women's Association also used fundraising as an impetus for a dinner – 'A Wild Foods Evening'. The C.W.A. ladies cooked and offered 'A Delicious Menu of Tantalising Rabbit and Venison with a Wild Foods Twist followed by Delicious Deserts'. The evening concluded with a talk on feral animals given by a Park Ranger and a silent auction of local produce. You don't get entertainment like that in the city.

THE MENAGERIE

'Listen to this Mum,' said my youngest kindergarten teacher daughter over the phone. I heard a sound like flip-flops on polished boards. 'What is it'? I said. 'Oh Mum, it's so cute! I am looking after a little duckling for the weekend.' 'What is it doing inside?' 'Running up and down the passage' (she didn't mention the other thing that little ducks do almost continually). Monday came and Duck-Duck went back to kindergarten where her future was discussed. The lovely Chinese cook was very keen to take her and get her nice and fat (I think pancakes and plum sauce may have been mentioned). You've guessed it. Next week Duck-Duck came to Picardy.

Owning a duck did cause a problem. By day at Picardy she roamed free, frequently hopping in the pond for a quick dip whenever the fancy took her and accompanying me whenever any digging was being done. By night she slept in the dovecote, which came to be called The Duckhouse ... but during the week, of course, we lived in the city. She became accustomed to travelling up and down in a cat box (Bossy Boots, the cat, preferred to sit on the back seat with Molly the dog anyway!). Poor Duck-Duck came to a sad end several years later when she became lunch for a visiting fox. She is remembered fondly. She was a loving and affectionate pet and good company in the garden.

LE PALAIS DE POULETS

Having now become poulterers we decided we should expand from one duck and purchase some chooks.

As we were weekenders their enclosure would have to be secure. We read up on deep-litter systems which, with automatic food and water dispensers, would enable us to keep them locked up all week and free-range them at the weekend. Influenced by the lovely henhouse at Montsalvat I designed a pretty little *Palais de Poulets*. The family rallied to the cause again and soon we had a little house with nesting boxes accessible from the outside. Our first family – a rooster and three hens – were a breed called Lace Winged Wyandottes: Henri, Henriette, Florette and Collette. It wasn't long before we had a broody hen and twenty-one days later, chicks: little tiny balls of yellow fluff. Very quickly they reached the gawky teenage years with stiff feathers appearing, and then their voices seemed to break. Was that the beginning of a 'cock-a-doodle-do'? An ad in the local paper – 'Free to a good home' – solved that little problem and after that we religiously removed the eggs every weekend (always checking carefully when cooking to make sure there wasn't extra protein).

When we were in residence the Wyandotte family free-ranged. One afternoon I was alerted by a ruckus in the garden and I looked out of the upstairs window to see a fox streaking through the paddock with Henri hanging from his mouth. I yelled out of the window and then tore down the stairs, but neither Henri nor the fox were anywhere to be seen. Henriette, Florette and Collette fussed around and were very happy to return to the *Palais*. As I bolted the door I looked up to see Henri racing back at full stretch, doing a very good imitation of Road Runner. He flew back in with his ladies who made a big fuss of him, clucking and commiserating.

The next day it was obvious that Henri had suffered an injury (he was using his beak as the third leg of a tripod). We decided we would give him some time to recover from his trauma during which his little harem never left his side. After some days we reluctantly decided that poor Henri should be put out of his misery. Bryce sharpened the axe, prepared the chopping block and lifted Henri out of the coop. Henri took one look at the gruesome preparations and took off at a fast clip. No sign of any disability. He returned to the *Palais* as usual that evening and life went on as before. This is a true story!

Eventually our Wyandotte family died from old age and we needed to replace them. Friends told us about a local poultry fanciers' club, which holds a sale once a month for members to sell their surplus birds. In a large shed in the show grounds we discovered rows and rows of cages one above the other and filled with every type of hen, rooster, duck, drake, turkey and goose, in our eyes, known to man. White-coated officials with stewards' badges bustled around, placing labels identifying the breeds on the cages – but with no mention of price. A sign on the wall warned us 'PLEASE – PLEASE – PLEASE – BE RESPECTFUL to the rights of other customers – NO PUSHING AND SHOVING' and that no sales were allowed before 10 a.m. Fortunately we met somebody who filled us in on the protocol. The deal was that after selecting the birds that piqued your interest, you took up position in front of the cage. At the ringing of the bell, on the dot of 10 a.m., stewards placed the prices on the cages and then it was 'first in best dressed'; the first one to snatch the card was the successful buyer. Standing next to us in front of our pick, 'Three Isa Brown Hens, at point of lay', was a statuesque lady with Brunhilda plaits and a determined demeanour. The bell rang, the card was placed and SNATCH. We didn't even see her hand move, and we went home from our first poultry sale empty-handed. There was no dispute. She had the fastest hands in the shed.

Our present Mademoiselles are a hotchpotch of breeds. There is Frou-Frou, a gold bantam with a bustle of black-tipped feathers; Lady Grey, a Light Sussex with a necklace of pale-grey feathers; Miss Maggie, an over-confident escapist with white bodice and black lace collar; and Rhonda the Redhead, an Isa Brown laying machine. They live happily in the Palais without a consort. (What you have never had you don't miss.)

ADDING TO THE MENAGERIE

We branched into livestock when, while visiting some sheep-farming friends, we came across an abandoned lamb in the paddock. The mother was nowhere to be seen. All day

I observed this lonely little lamb. It was Sunday and our friends, also weekenders, were heading back to Melbourne. I couldn't just leave him in the paddock to the mercy of foxes, so that is how I came to adopt a day-old lamb. To this day Bryce claims I stole him from his mother while she was off having a drink at the trough.

Lucciano Lambino took to his bottle and settled happily in the laundry. Monday morning came and into the car went Lucciano in a box on the floor; on the passenger seat, Molly the dog to keep the lamb in the box; and Bossy Boots the cat and Duck-Duck (in the cat box) took the rear seat. This arrangement worked quite well for a few weeks, but then Lucciano started to graze grass as well as take his bottle. Our garden in Melbourne was minute and he soon polished off the small patch of lawn. He looked so chic in his little red collar and lead when I took him to the local park to graze. One day on my way back to Picardy I returned to the car after paying for petrol to find Molly sitting up behind the wheel in the driver's seat, Lucciano standing on the passenger seat and the duck and the cat in their usual spots. A man filling his car at the next-door bowser was staring as if he couldn't believe his eyes. If only I had had the wit at the time to get in the back seat with the others and say 'Drive on!' Lucciano was promptly weaned and became a full-time grass-grazing resident at Picardy.

My daughter's horse, Cherokee, was also a full-time resident. He had served his time as a pony club horse and then at a city children's farm where our daughter taught riding. He was now a contented retiree with nothing to do and too much to eat (a common problem for many retirees). To help keep his eating problem under control we fenced off a pony paddock where he stood for hours gazing up the road watching for the infrequent traffic. His paddock adjoined the drive where we had decided to plant Lombardy poplars. He watched with interest as we dug the holes and planted the top side. Running out of daylight hours (which we often did when we were weekenders), we leaned the remaining trees against the fence – his fence – to plant the following morning. When we returned the next day to resume planting our once-tall poplars were now level with the top strand of barbed wire. It could have been possums, but I doubt it. Despite this setback these trees quickly caught up with the other side.

5 Meandering

The arrival of the menagerie – and all this lovely manure from the Wyandotte family, Duck-Duck, Lucciano, Cherokee and the visiting cows – got us thinking about making a new garden. Why not more roses, for instance? The purchase of a ride-on mower gave more scope to my ideas and in no time at all a meandering path was mown behind the pond rose garden, across the short walk, behind the pink rose bed, across the rose arbour, behind the apricot bed ... and we began to make new beds on the other side of the path. I had learnt my lesson with double digging. This time, after mowing closely, I covered the soil with wads of newspaper that lined The Duckhouse floor every night. I covered the paper with a thick layer of grass clippings, then (once it had all rotted down) planted directly into the soil with the minimum of digging.

As the garden 'moved away' from the house the shapes became more informal. Once again the natural topography to a certain extent dictated the sizes of the beds, and by not double digging the beds tended to grow wider. This encouraged me to choose bigger growing roses. At the north end of the meandering path I began with *Rosa semi-plena*, the white rose of York, then the beautiful pale-lemon yellow almost-single 'Golden Wings'. Jostling aside the roses is the Californian tree poppy, *Romneya coulteri*, the large flowers looking like gorgeous poached eggs made of white crêpe paper. Making a tall bendy open shrub is 'Dupontii', a single creamy-white species rose, flowering only in spring. Squashed in beside her is prickly old pink 'Sarah Van Fleet' from the Rugosa family. She has since been overrun by a self-sown single-pink rambler. Directly in front of the rose arbour is a shrub, *Cotinus coggryia*, the smoke bush, a deciduous shrub with ruddy autumn-coloured leaves and flowers that form dusty-pink clouds. Growing through and over the top of this shrub is the China rose, 'Mutabilis' with its ragged, multi-coloured blooms of yellow, pink and crimson. Next in line is 'Variegata di Bologna' a puce-and-white striped rose and behind her is the wine-red 'Chianti'. The next rose, 'Sadlers Wells', is a bit of a ring in – a frilly single, rather garish pinky-red with a white centre – although she does match perfectly the centranthus at her feet. She is here because we have come to the 'dress circle': a small oval of grass, encircled with Ballerina roses which have clusters of single pink-and-white centred blooms.

Stepping off the meandering path and into the dress circle there is a gap which leads to an open, roughly circular area of grass with an ornamental cherry as a centrepoint. The cherry has a lovely wide spreading shape, the striated bark is very beautiful and the autumn colour is good, but the blossom is very disappointing – a case of mislabelling. What was meant to be *Prunus shirotae*, or 'Mt Fuji,' with pure-white blossom, is a nondescript bruise-pink. My eldest daughter, in the early stages of a much-wanted pregnancy, spent days plotting and marking out the complicated shape for the hedge which now encloses this cherry lawn.

Back on the meandering path, curving behind the pond garden is a fence covered with a climbing rose – which to me has no name other than 'The Old Church Rose' – given to me by a friend who took a cutting from an old churchyard. It is probably one of the most prolific bloomers in the whole garden. Gorgeous perfume, lovely shaped, deep-pink flowers which repeat again and again from spring to late autumn.

You can never have too much of a good thing.

Over time more free-form beds appeared heading down towards the creek, as having given double digging away now we just mowed a new path in the pasture, often following a path where previously cattle had trod. In addition to roses we planted several varieties of viburnum, lilacs, a persimmon tree and more cotinus. I played with colour matching the red rose 'The Prince' and the lovely 'White Wings', with its white single petals and a boss of red stamens, with burgundy-leafed cotinus. Yellow was my theme in another section using the single-species rose 'Canary Bird', 'Golden Wings' and 'Graham Thomas', underplanted with yellow day lilies and other yellow bits and pieces. Bryce insisted it was time to build a permanent fence to stop the garden sprawl. Until this time we had optimistically kept the agisted cows out of the garden with a single hot-wire electric fence. Dairy cows are very docile and obedient but beef cattle less so.

One week I was spending time at Picardy in preparation for a garden opening the following weekend. Bonbon, our miniature Dachshund, and I were dozing in front of the open fire after dinner when she suddenly fell into a paroxysm of barking. Shading my eyes with cupped hands I peered out the window into the darkness and looking straight back at me were many pairs of bovine eyes. The gravel forecourt in front of the house was full of cattle. Not really believing my eyes I turned on the outside light. With a bit of a kick and a head toss fortunately the whole herd turned and walked sedately down the drive. Imagine what thirty-five head of cattle could have done?! It wasn't the fault of the electric fence, but an open gate.

A LITTLE GARDEN GNOME

We were beginning to receive requests to open our garden to small bus tours and garden clubs, and then a local nursery planned a big rose weekend. We needed help and that was how, Lorna, our little garden gnome, began to come every Monday morning to garden with me and to enrich our lives with her wonderful stories and unfailing good humour. At first I was apprehensive because some time before her joining us she had passed three score and ten, but after our first morning together any doubts went out the window. She was a tiny blue-eyed, white-haired dynamo. We began by weeding a bed, throwing the weeds onto a large tarpaulin. When we had amassed a nice big pile we each took hold of a corner and began to drag it towards the compost heap in the paddock. Lorna set off at a fast clip and I found I had to run to keep up with her. Not to be outdone she broke into a trot too. She was as fit as a fiddle.

Over time the stories of her rich and interesting life began to be revealed. Her mother, a former ballet dancer, had died when Lorna was quite young and she and her sister had grown up with an unconventional father surrounded by horses and animals. She became a very talented child violinist who had come to the attention of Yehudi Menuhin, and in later years was involved in Melbourne's theatrical world playing in the role of a soubrette. To help support herself she worked part-time as a gardener in various Toorak gardens.

She told me a story of going to England as a bright young thing and attending the Ascot races. A flurry of people came in to where her party was sitting and she piped up, 'You can't come in here. This is the Royal Enclosure.' She was very quickly shushed by her escort as Princess Margaret and her entourage were ushered to their seats.

In later years she became enamoured with Spanish flamenco dancing and took herself to Spain to learn the art. She must have been an exceptional pupil as she returned to Melbourne and started a Spanish dancing troupe. Her stage name was Caramina. The troupe toured overseas and performed at Carnegie Hall in New York. Closer to home they performed regularly at Montsalvat at Eltham, and I took her back there one day to visit. She was thrilled when the current owner, Sigmund Jorgenson, remembered their performances.

By the time Lorna came into our lives she lived in a little house called Rose Cottage with her dog, many cats, hens and three horses. Her cats lived in a special

chicken-wired room built onto the house. She maintained a 2-acre garden of roses, fruit trees and vegetables and spent three days a week gardening for others. In her spare time she taught violin at the local school and most afternoons took students at home.

We were invited to a musical afternoon at a friend's house where Lorna and her friend were to perform. We were a little late and the performance had begun. After a short break they were persuaded to begin again. 'Now where were we?' said Lorna. 'About two pages ahead of me!' replied the friend. That accurately sums up Lorna: always ahead of the game.

Lorna helped in the garden well into her eighties and I am deeply grateful for what she taught me about gardening – 'If it's not pretty, pull it out' – and her example of how to live life.

We were thrilled to be invited to her ninetieth birthday party and to meet her Spanish dancing partner of earlier years, and to hear more of her life's stories from a hall full of people whose lives had also been enriched by her presence.

'SIZZLEHURST CRESCENT', THE EMPTY ROOM AND THE DOGWOOD WALK

A friend gave Bryce a tree for a big birthday. 'It's that tree that's in that famous white garden in the UK – Sizzlehurst I think it's called,' he said. The tree in question was *Pyrus salicifolia*, known as a weeping silver pear. At Sissinghurst, a small statue of The Little Virgin shelters underneath the branches. At Picardy a rather more wanton wench, who we have named Chloe, slouches provocatively underneath our tree. She is a reproduction of a series of sculptures depicting the seasons. She is spring and her little rounded tum, *deshabillé* and smirky smile seem to suggest that she is indeed a little goddess of fertility and fecundity. In her honour and as a tribute to the great garden we planted a hedge around the tree to form Sizzlehurst Crescent.

We were having a lot of success with growing hedges of privet from cuttings and Bryce was proving to be a hedge clipper *extraordinaire*, so cubes of hedge were formed to hide the posts that supported the espaliers. We continued these around a nice flat rectangle of grass – a croquet lawn perhaps? – but now more prosaically called the 'empty room' or 'the wedding lawn'. It would make a lovely spot for a swimming pool, which is highly unlikely to happen on our watch. It does make a nice breathing space in the middle of a busy garden.

At this point the meandering path joins the dogwood walk: a collection of pink and white dogwoods, *Cornus kousa*, *chinensis* and *florida* and evergreen, summer-flowering, pale-chartreuse *Cornus capitata*. The flowering season of dogwoods is much longer than other blossom trees as the 'flowers' are really bracts rather than petals. As the bracts age the colours fade from dark pink to a pale shell-pink. Before the leaves colour in autumn the trees are festooned with red fruit, which last till the birds discover them. Underplanted with hellebores, cyclamens, bluebells and other bulbs this area is now very pretty in early spring.

THE OVAL

Most of our property slopes away to the creek but there is a flat knoll where cattle have always camped at night. It seemed a perfect spot for playing cricket and kicking a footy away from the garden. I bought a handful of elm seedlings from a market stall and when I divided them up I discovered there were exactly eleven plants. These eleven seedlings that we planted around the edge of The Oval are now big trees and named after past members of English cricket teams – 'forever banished to the boundary'. Among them we have 'Beefy' Botham, thickset and solid; David Gower, tall and elegant; Gladstone Small, diminutive and 'with little or no neck' as described by the English commentator Christopher Martin-Jenkins; and last but not least Geoffrey Boycott, slow to leaf. Overlooking The Oval we have a special wisteria-shaded seat in memory of a dear friend of the family, Sally.

'Mowing' The Oval now keeps our grandchildren entertained when they visit. When they were very little they sat on our laps as we mowed and then, for a time, as they graduated to solo driving under close supervision, they drove round and round in circles achieving nothing as they were too light to activate the blades. Now they are growing up they do a good job with the mowing.

When we are harvesting the grapes the job of driving the mower, with trailer attached, to ferry the tubs of grapes to the barn for crushing is given to the grandchildren, freeing up the adult hands for picking. Much more fun than picking.

The eldest will soon be old enough to begin driving lessons so the appeal of our 'wheels' will, I am sure, diminish – but the younger ones still fight to have a turn.

6 Building the barn

The dormitory in the house was getting a little cosy as new members were added to the family, and we began to think about building a barn to provide extra accommodation. After our experimental build of the dovecote we knew that building a barn ourselves was out of the question. We heard about a company manufacturing traditional heavy timber frames, assembled by mortice-and-tenon joints, reminiscent of the old oak-framed buildings of Europe. Mud-brick builders in Australia usually sourced old recycled timber which was becoming harder to find and expensive. This company used freshly milled Radiata pine. Their theory was that the now-old frames in Europe that have lasted hundreds of years had, when first built, been made of green oak. The mortice-and-tenon joints allowed the green timber to move and settle as it aged. As extra protection the timber is not exposed on the outside (as in the usual mud-brick building method) but exposed on the inside of the mud walls. The frames were designed in modules, which could be arranged to suit your purpose.

We designed a large open room with two bedrooms, mezzanine and a bathroom upstairs. The huge frames were delivered to the site pre-cut and pre-morticed. It was suggested that it would be easier to paint the frames while they were lying on the ground so I mixed up a limewash tinted with a bit of ochre and sloshed it on. The frames were then assembled like a giant toy building set and with the aid of a 4WD pulled up into place, just like an Amish barn raising. A crew of 'muddies' then came to complete the walls, which rose a lot more quickly than The Duckhouse had.

We sourced some old iron-framed windows for the ground floor and had arched ones made to match. I found two pairs of old wooden doors – one pair from an old stable in South Melbourne and the other, I am sure, came from a church as they still have a 'churchy' smell. In Collingwood I found a black cast-iron four-oven Metter's woodstove – I cannot resist a stove – and an old fish-and-chip-shop cowl which formed the base for the large fireplace chimneypiece. We celebrated the near completion of the barn – no walls upstairs – on Millennium night with a sit-down dinner with friends and family.

Over time we have made a collection of old farm tools and implements which hang on the whitewashed walls. The worn wooden handles from old bow saws, scythes and various pitchforks, spades and shovels tell a story of how physically hard the work was

in earlier days on farms before chainsaws, front-end loaders and mowers were available. They are also beautifully made and worthy of hanging on the walls as a piece of art. They remind me of my father's stories of his early days on our farm in Western Australia where teams of horses were used to plough, seed and harvest. Before the day's work could begin he rose at 4 a.m. to feed, water and harness the team. He was one of the first farmers in the area to purchase a new-fangled iron-wheeled tractor when they became available.

His life on the farm, on reflection, was terribly hard to begin with. For the first few years he lived in a 'humpy' made from corrugated iron, his bed at one end, raised from the dirt floor on the wooden tray from a dray. His cupboards were made out of Rose's kerosene tins and wooden fruit boxes. At the other end of the room were a small woodstove and a large wooden bench, which was both workbench and kitchen table. There was no refrigerator, just a 'Coolgardie safe', a zinc-box contraption with perforated metal walls and hessian sides which 'cooled' by water evaporation. Fresh meat didn't remain fresh very long so he ran a large number of hens and roosters for eggs and meat. Eventually his flock of poultry became so numerous that the farm was known locally as Cackleberry Farm. He told a story that one summer chickens had hatched from eggs that were sitting in a bowl on his kitchen bench without the assistance of a hen.

By the time my mother arrived as a new bride he had built a three-room weatherboard house a little distance from the 'humpy'. It must have seemed like a palace to him: all mod cons, kerosene refrigerator, one cold tap in the kitchen and so on. I am not sure what my mother thought, coming from a large brick house in a prosperous town in South Australia. By the time my memories of the farm begin the 'humpy' had been relegated to being the blacksmith forge where he mended bits and pieces, still by our standards primitive as this was pre-welding days. Eventually it returned to its origins and became a part of the hen enclosure before it finally fell down after being hit by a willy-willy.

WASTE NOT, WANT NOT

Perhaps these stories that I was raised on but never really experienced have influenced me more than I realise, because whenever we finished a project at Picardy there always seemed to be a pile of leftover materials – 'Pity to waste those bricks and we have no way of taking them to the tip' – so a bread oven was added to the list of things to build. Books

were again consulted and a design decided on, and over some weeks the oven grew. The critical part of an oven is the domed top. A carpenter friend made us a lathe frame on which to build the dome. The construction is of brick halves wedged with broken brick fragments to fit the curve of the frame. This sounded complicated, and I had doubts that it would work. My son and I tentatively began mortaring in the wedged bricks layer by layer around the frame. Eureka! It worked. When dry the dome was rendered and then left to cure. Finally the day came to light the oven. Other than the odd tack from the lathe frame in the pizza it was pronounced a great success.

THE PERGOLA

To link the house to the barn it was decided to build a pergola using the same size timbers as used in the barn frame. Our engineer son was of the opinion that the weight of the timbers was too great to be lifted manually, and suggested that we hire a crane. Faced with this extra cost Bryce and a friend worked out a solution. Using two ladders as supports they lifted the timbers rung by rung until they were in the right position. White wisteria, clematis and the rose 'Lamarque' soon covered the new pergola, which provides a cool shady breezeway in summer.

7 The produce department

Finishing off the barn, rendering the outside and whitewashing the interior took some months to complete.

While all this was going on we were also working on new projects in the garden.

THE VINEYARD

On the north side of the house was a large area of grass pasture in which for a long time we allowed the cows to graze, almost to the edge of the brick-paved terrace. We wished to keep this space open and simple because the views of the countryside and open sky were very important to us. As we often sat on our ornamental grapevine-covered terrace in the evenings enjoying a glass of wine it occurred to Bryce that it would be nice to grow our own grapes. Our son was also interested in having a vineyard, so father and son visited various vineyards, sampling varieties they thought suited to our climate.

In the words of the viticulturist father:

'There were a few vineyards in our area growing Shiraz and Pinot Noir but we decided to try some different varieties – Sangiovese – an Italian red variety used in Chianti, and 'Pinot Gris', a French white grape. In preparation for planting we had the soil deep-ripped, then a contractor put in the trellising and we ordered our 220 vines. Six rows of each variety. Almost as an afterthought we booked ourselves in to a "Small Scale Viticulture" course, and in late August 2001 we planted our vineyard.

'Over the next three years the vines received loving care – hand weeding rather than chemical weed control – and pruning and training onto the fruiting wires to ensure maximum production. To prepare ourselves for the next step we attended a winemaking course, experimented with grapes bought from a wholesale market and started to invest in our equipment needed to turn grape juice into wine. Now every year the cycle repeats. Winter pruning, spring spraying every ten days for mould, bud thinning, hedging the canopy and finally netting the whole vineyard to prevent bird damage. Berry testing for ripeness begins in late February and picking starts with the Pinot Gris mid-March and the Sangiovese early April. The berries are processed in the barn. The red Sangiovese goes through a crusher de-stemmer, fermenting tank, basket press and finally into a stainless-steel tank. The white Pinot Gris is a faster process: crusher de-stemmer, basket press

"Picardy"
2014
"Picardy"

and then stainless-steel tank. Dry ice is used in the tank to cool the Pinot Gris juice as quickly as we can to keep the flavour crisp. During the year as the wine matures the wine is racked – pumped from one tank to another several times – and then bottled, the Pinot Gris in August and the Sangiovese in February, just before we need the tanks for the next vintage. To store our wine we have built a cellar by excavating into the bank of earth behind the barn. Fitted by a heavy solid timber door we can now keep our wine at a cool constant temperature to mature.

'Grape picking and bottling and labelling days now involve three generations of the family, plus friends. On picking days it's all hands on deck: the adults pick and the grandchildren take turns driving the mower with the trailer full of tubs of grapes to the barn where they are crushed. We have developed our own traditions. Grapepickers' cake at mid-morning is now essential, and our long vintage lunch always includes fat pork sausages with fennel, cooked in the freshly crushed must.'

THE OLIVE GROVE

The vineyard had not taken up all the space to the north of the house, so lower down the hill we planted a small grove of mixed olive varieties. Some of these have proved to be very productive and others only ornamental. It is very satisfying to eat our own olives while drinking our own wine at aperitif time. As another little tribute to France every spring we grow a plot of red Flanders poppies (*coquelicot*) between the vineyard and the olives.

Nearby a circle of wild olive seedlings, gathered in the Barossa Valley from our daughter-in-law's family farm, are clipped into a Rubenesque-shaped hedge to mirror the sensually rounded hills in the background and form a windbreak for the rest of the garden.

THE VEGETABLE GARDEN

Like anyone who has ever visited that vegetable garden to end all vegetable gardens – Villandry, in France – I too had aspirations to emulate it on a smaller scale. We dug beds in the mown grass and I planted in patterns, by colour matching and by colour contrasts. The problem was when you harvested it spoiled the patterns. I tried inter-planting and at staggered times so that every second lettuce (theoretically) would be ready at the same time. The lettuces didn't seem to get the hang of it.

I have discovered over the years that growing vegetables is more difficult than growing flowers. The soil needs to be very fertile, constantly built up with organic matter and a fine tilth. Sowing seeds or planting seedlings of the right variety at the right time and in the right season is critical. They need to grow fast, must have lots of water to be successful and need to be picked as soon as they are ready and – the bit I find difficult – you have to be prepared to spoil the picture. When I was studying horticulture I was told to factor in the time it takes for harvesting the produce. I thought that was ridiculous – surely you just pick it when it's ready? – but it is true. How much produce has gone to the hens because I haven't had time to pick it at its peak! Like any plant, vegetables have one ambition, and that is to grow and set seed to reproduce. That's fine if you are growing peas or beans, but not so good if they are leafy vegetables.

Our present and final vegetable garden next to the *Palais de Poulets* is much smaller with wooden-edged beds, and we try to grow only what we can eat. That means one zucchini plant only! Of course I still want it to be pretty and love growing purple runner beans, very productive and disease-free, with yellow bush butter beans at their feet and other combinations. In summer a packet of inexpensive zinnia seeds gives us a blaze of colour, like a box of Smarties, in any empty spots.

Red cabbage is a winter 'must have' and lasts a long time in the garden. We find it to be easier to grow than green cabbage, which seems to be more susceptible to the cabbage moth. Chinese cabbage takes less time to mature than drum head cabbage, takes up less space, is slow to bolt, grows all year round and is delicious.

Last winter I grew a mixed bed of cauliflowers and broccoli. Broccoli is higher yielding because of the side shoots, but it is still a thrill to pick a snowy head of cauliflower. I also love to grow peas, but confess I often forget to pick them – frozen peas are just too easy. Young broad beans, double peeled, we love cooked with a little of our son's home-made pancetta. Artichokes, if you pick them when small, are also delicious but you must be ruthless with trimming off the outer leaves down to the pale-green centre. If left to flower they make a giant purple thistle flower and are very striking. Silver beet is a great standby. The rainbow variety looks fantastic, but I think 'Fordhook Giant' is better for eating.

WINTER–SPRING

The queen of this season is asparagus. Our asparagus bed is now twenty years old. The secret is to prepare the bed really well by digging a trench 60-centimetres deep and layering with manure and soil, keeping the topsoil till last and then planting the crowns 10 centimetres deep. Do not bother with those punnets of feathery seedlings unless you are very young and have time to wait! Try to find mature crowns which look a bit like the roots of agapanthus – long white fingers. Do not be tempted to cut the spears the first year. They will grow into tall fronds, so let them die back in autumn before trimming, and cut lightly for the first few years. Most importantly, plant three times as many as you think you should. I have read that you can control weeds in the bed with salt. I know asparagus grows wild in areas of high salinity, so it may be correct.

My favourite way of eating asparagus is boiled very briefly in a little salted water then doused in olive oil, a good squeeze of lemon juice and showered with freshly ground pepper. It's nice also as 'soldiers' with a soft-boiled egg in a pretty eggcup.

SUMMER–AUTUMN

Our summer–autumn vegetable garden is dominated by the tomato. The perfume of tomato leaves is so evocative of summer. Truly a Proustian moment. Unless it is a really hot summer we have trouble ripening tomatoes early. My choice for an all-round performer is the variety 'Rouge Marmande', and we always have some small cherry tomatoes, often self-sown. Basil, a tomato's best friend, is always nearby. In our early years we tried to grow enough tomatoes to make Italian tomato sauce for pasta. Now I find it more convenient to buy boxes of plum tomatoes when there is a glut.

Lettuce is also a must have for summer, and the trick is to get the demand to match the supply. Often we have lettuce bolting and running to seed because we have planted too many at the one time. When this happens they often sprout small secondary leaves. I just add a bit more Dijon mustard to the dressing to counteract any bitterness. The leaves can also be gently cooked in a little butter with some finely chopped onion and frozen peas; delicious with lamb or chicken.

CITRUS AND SOFT FRUIT

In our small grove of mixed citrus varieties we have blood and navel oranges, tangelos, grapefruit, lime and lemons: all extremely productive over a long period of time. They

are very ornamental with beautiful glossy dark-green foliage contrasting with the bright globes of fruit. When in blossom the perfume fills the air and our daily ration of freshly squeezed juice does, I believe, keep us in tip-top health.

Raspberries are easy to grow in our cool climate if you can protect them from birds. Any surplus freezes well, either made into a coulis or as whole fruit. If freezing whole spread on a tray in a single layer, freeze and then tip into plastic containers to store. They should stay loose. Loganberries also grow well here. Unfortunately the birds love them as much as we do.

Strawberries like fertile, slightly acidic soil. The best strawberries we have ever grown were mulched with pine needles and irrigated with 'ducky' water syphoned from the rose garden pond. They make a lovely edge to an ornamental garden, and if close to the house your furry friends may scare and keep the birds away so that nets are not necessary. Our miniature Dachshund, Bonbon, made it her business to never let a bird near our strawberries. The pretty little *fraises de bois* – wood strawberries – appear in odd places all over the garden and are the absolute essence of strawberry scent and flavour.

We also have an English mulberry tree which, until last year, the birds ignored, but the English blackbirds have now discovered that too. The fruit is delicious. The fruit of the damson plum is highly decorative with a white bloom on the deep-purple skin, giving an iridescent bluish caste. Cooked in a crumble the colour is a magnificent ruby-red. I suspect that with their tart flavour they would also make a great accompaniment to roast duck, taking the place of the more usual cherries.

Figs are also easy to grow but once again here we have to net, which is a nuisance when picking. A fruit cage would be wonderful. It has just occurred to me that a multi-purpose walk-in fruit-cage-cum-hen-run might work, solving two problems – birds and foxes – food for thought!

Do not plant a fig tree near your house. They have a terrible smell reminiscent of tomcats.

THE WILD GARDEN AND TRUFFERIE

With the demise of Cherokee, the horse paddock became available. Previously we had thought of creating a nuttery, *à la* Gertrude Jekyll, but decided that we were already providing enough food for the local parrot population. Instead we decided to make a woodland area and hoped to create the lacy-leafed dappled effect of a French forest.

We chose *Robinnia decaisneana*, a grafted pale-pink variety with trusses of beautiful wisteria-like flowers. We planted randomly, leaving a space for a pathway. They grew quickly and before many years had achieved the effect we wanted. Robinnias have a habit of suckering which in this particular situation suits us well. The suckers have creamy white flowers which blend beautifully with the pink, and in late October the perfume and the picture are sublime

For autumn colour we have *Parrotia persica*, red maples, amelanchier, *Cotinus purpurea* and a liquid amber. We have underplanted with Spanish bluebells, which have quickly multiplied and have added silver birches, white *Magnolia stellata* and white, pink and yellow daffodils. Violets, purple, pink and white are spreading and creating a weed-suppressing ground cover. The trees are gradually out-competing the wild grasses, and after the bulbs have died down we mow the grass for summer. This area is now one of our favourite parts of the garden.

Our last big area to be developed – up to this point in time! – was the trufferie. Bryce was celebrating another major birthday and friends were asking me for gift ideas for the garden. I was struggling with what to suggest when I read an article about farmed truffles. Just what any French-themed fantasy worth its salt should have!

I made enquiries and sourced from Tasmania oak seedlings inoculated with truffle spores. Each guest presented him with a small plastic pot with a 3-inch tree, some still with acorn attached. Truffles grow wild in France in areas of naturally occurring limestone with a pH of 8 to 9. Our pH reading is 6.5 –7, and so a lot of lime was necessary to correct this. When the large truck arrived the driver was nonplussed when shown the small area which was to be top-dressed with lime. I could read his mind: 'Bloody hobby farmers!' In ten years the seedlings have grown into big trees, but needless to say we have not yet harvested a truffle.

8 Cooking and carousing

One of the many delights of living at Picardy is entertaining family and friends. Since we have been here we have grown from a family of five to fourteen, and occasionally we all get together to put our feet under the table, usually at Christmas time. We set up the Christmas tree and the big table in the barn and the family arrives for lunch, a casual affair of present opening, champagne, nibbles, prawn and mango salad and the first slices of the ham. After forty winks I crank up the big woodstove in the barn to cook the full Christmas catastrophe, turkey with all the trimmings for dinner in the cool of the evening. Dessert may be *bûche de Noël*, summer pudding or, now that our grandchildren like to cook, chocolate fondant pudding. The traditional plum pudding has in later years been given the thumbs down and now we make a sticky date pudding in the same basin with the same threepenny bits that my mother used to put in her traditional plum pudding. The threepenny bits are counted as they go into the pudding, and an audit is conducted at the end of the meal.

With the first rains of autumn we begin to look out for field mushrooms. We have observed that the mushrooms are more plentiful after a hot summer. What could be better than a few friends at the table, some thick fillet steaks from the local butcher, a black, rich, unctuous mushroom sauce, the last of the green runner beans and a buttery potato mash? Add in some red wine, our Sangiovese or our neighbours' Pinot Noir, and we are truly kings in grass castles.

In winter, during the long weekend in June, there is a birthday to celebrate, the wine is ready to rack and it is cold enough to make charcuterie. Our son is in charge of this activity. The barn is a hive of activity and noise and redolent with new wine, garlic and spices for the salted pork, simmering Napoli sauce and the yeasty smell of rising pizza dough. Grandsons keep the pizza oven stoked. By lunchtime the pork is tightly rolled in its casing, trussed with string and hanging in a dark cool corner to air dry. Depending on the cut of pork we will have coppocollo, pancetta and salami later in the year.

Late in summer, when Roma or plum tomatoes are cheap and plentiful, we turn our hand to sauce making. (Another excuse to gather a group of friends together in the

barn.) Over the years we have collected beer bottles that are capped with crown seals (these are becoming rare as screw caps are now used). Jobs are allocated. A team to wash and sterilise bottles, another to blanch the tomatoes briefly in boiling water, then cut them in half and set them to drain. Blanching serves two purposes – one, to kill off any moulds and so on which may affect the sauce later and two, to soften the skins. The tomato halves are then put through a device which separates skins and pips from the flesh. Initially we used a hand-cranked machine, but the next generation have invested in an electric one which makes the process a lot quicker, but with a certain loss of romance. The juicy flesh – the passata – is now poured into the bottles, basil may be added, sealed and packed into an old copper or drum and set over a gas burner (or more rustically over a wood fire) and brought to a rolling boil for two hours. The bottles remain in the water until cool enough to handle safely. This sauce is thinnish and is used in cooking pasta sauces and meat dishes. If the tomatoes are cooked before passing through the separator the sauce will be thicker. Of course, at the end of the day large quantities of pasta and home-made red wine are consumed by the team.

THE DIRT ROAD DINNER CLUB

In our early days there were not many restaurants nearby, and as I love to cook the barn became a pop-up restaurant for friends and neighbours. We called ourselves The Dirt Road Dinner Club. The dinners were composed around the seasons and special events. We have celebrated the seasons, New Year's Eves, Australia Day, Bastille Day and had an Easter Sunday breakfast ... and have gathered at other times for no particular reason other than we just felt like getting together. I have a lot of fun devising the themes, menus and decorating the long table in the barn. These dinners have satisfied (and cured) a long-held yen to run a food establishment of my own.

SAMPLE MENUS

Summer – long lazy days
Tartelette of slow-roasted tomato with goat's cheese and basil-infused oil
Quail wrapped in proscuitto with Pinot Gris grapes
Cheese
Peach melba

Autumn – a walk on the wild side
Soft curd goat's cheese with a wild fennel flower dressing, figs and wild Barossa olives
Chestnut gnocchi with brown butter and crisp sage leaves.
Braised rabbit with field mushrooms and truffle-scented semolina
Bush honey panna cotta with poached quince and new season walnuts

Winter – Bastille Day Dinner
Aperitifs: Rillettes de lapin, radis au beurre au sel rose
Entrée: Salade chaud de betterave roti au fromage bleu, noix au vinaigrette
Plat Principal: Cassoulet de Toulouse
Dessert: Quenelles de tangelo crème brûlée aux salade de citrons

Spring – a picnic among the roses
Asparagus with egg mayonnaise
Poussin chicken with a Dijon mustard crust
Crisp potatoes and green salad
Strawberry tarts and cream

Australia Day 26 January – old Aussie favourites
Chilled spiced pumpkin soup with prawns
Pie of fillet steak and caramelised onions with mushy peas and
home-made tomato sauce
Pavlova 'en pointe'

I served this dish as an entrée when nouvelle cuisine was at its most fashionable: a small portion of food artistically arranged on a plate, often with two stalks of chives elegantly crossed on top. Scallops at the time were $8 a kilo in the markets.

Read through the recipe carefully and prepare all ingredients before starting to cook, as the faster it is assembled the better. Set out hot plates ready for speedy plating.

Scallops with orange beurre blanc and baby beans

(serves 4)

Ingredients

3-5 scallops per person, with orange roe intact

salt and pepper

olive oil

1 large glass (180-200ml) dry white wine

2 tablespoons strained fresh orange juice

few whole peppercorns

orange peel, long strip without pith

3 shallots or ½ onion, peeled and chopped very finely

1 tablespoon thick cream, 45 per cent butterfat

200g cold unsalted butter, cut into 8 pieces

3-4 spears of thin asparagus trimmed to 10cm lengths per person, or a small handful of 10cm-long green baby beans with the ends pinched off

Method

Leave the orange roe on the scallops but trim off any dark veins and fibre.

Rinse quickly under cold running water in a strainer and dry on paper towels, then put in a bowl.

Season with a little salt and pepper, and add about 1 tablespoon olive oil.

Mix, place on a paper-towel-covered plate to absorb any liquid and cover with cling wrap. Refrigerate till needed.

Sauce

In a small enamelled or stainless steel saucepan simmer white wine, orange juice, peppercorns, orange peel, shallots or onion until the liquid is almost evaporated and shallots or onion are soft and moist.

Remove the peppercorns and orange peel.

Add the cream and bring to the boil.

Remove from the heat and whisk in the butter, one piece at a time, adding another as the first is absorbed. Work quickly, but if the butter stops being amalgamated return to a gentle heat and whisk till a creamy consistency is reached. Taste, and season with salt if necessary. Keep warm by standing the pan in a container of hot, not boiling, water. Stir occasionally.

To cook

Bring a saucepan of salted water to a rolling boil and preheat a heavy cast iron frying pan or grill plate to very hot.

Oil the scallops lightly.

Without crowding the pan, sear the scallops quickly in batches till a golden colour on both sides.

Reheat the pan between batches if necessary; if not seared the scallops will weep liquid.

At the same time cook the asparagus or beans in the boiling water until just cooked, but still with a crunch. Drain.

To assemble

Place scallops in the centre of each warmed plate.

Scatter a jumble of beans on the top.

With a spoon drizzle over the orange sauce and rush to the table.

TIP

The trick to this dish is preparation. Scallops and beans trimmed, and hot plates laid out on the bench ready for plating. The sauce can be made just before the guests arrive, but the scallops and beans are cooked at the last minute.

It is a good idea to have your guests seated at the table and busy with some nice bread and a glass of wine while all this activity is taking place, and to have something you've cooked the previous day heating gently in the oven for the next course!

The joy of an Aga stove is that the ovens are always hot and ready to go. The top oven is used for roasting, and the bottom oven for long slow cooking. The ovens are deep, and two baking dishes can slide in one behind the other so that potatoes can be cooked at the same time as the meat. The idea for this dish came from an American cookbook, but I believe its origins lie with Swedish immigrants.

Roast leg of lamb with a mustard and brown sugar crust with coffee gravy

(serves 6)

Ingredients

1 leg of lamb

olive oil

salt and pepper

dry English mustard powder or Dijon mustard

dark brown sugar

root vegetables (1-2 carrots, 1 large onion) cut in approx. 5cm chunks to flavour the gravy

approx. 2 tablespoons plain flour

strong black instant coffee (2 teaspoons diluted per cup of water)

potatoes, peeled and cut into 5cm chunks - quantities depend on appetite!

olive oil

Method

Preheat the oven to 200°C (400°F, gas mark 6).

Rub a little olive oil all over the lamb. Sprinkle with salt and a grind of black pepper and dust generously with dry mustard powder, or spread evenly and thinly with Dijon mustard.

With your hands firmly pat on a thick layer of brown sugar to cover the lamb.

Lightly grease a heavy baking dish, one that will be OK on a hot plate (to make the coffee gravy).

Place the lamb in the dish and surround with the vegetables. Roast for approx. 40 mins per kilo. Cover loosely with foil if the sugar begins to burn too much.

When the lamb is cooked, remove from the pan and place on a carving platter. Leave the lamb in a warm place lightly covered with foil. Discard the vegetables.

If there is a lot of fat in the baking dish pour it off, leaving enough liquid to make a roux by sifting a little flour into the liquid and stirring until smooth.

Return the baking dish to the hot plate and gently brown the roux. Add any juices from the rested meat (see Tip Box). Slowly add hot black coffee to the pan, stirring or whisking till you make an unctuous gravy. If the gravy is too thin keep boiling to reduce; if too thick add more black coffee. Taste – it may need salt and pepper. (Sometimes I add a tiny splash of vinegar just to sharpen the sauce.) Juices from the rested meat may be added to the sauce, but be careful not to add too much fat.

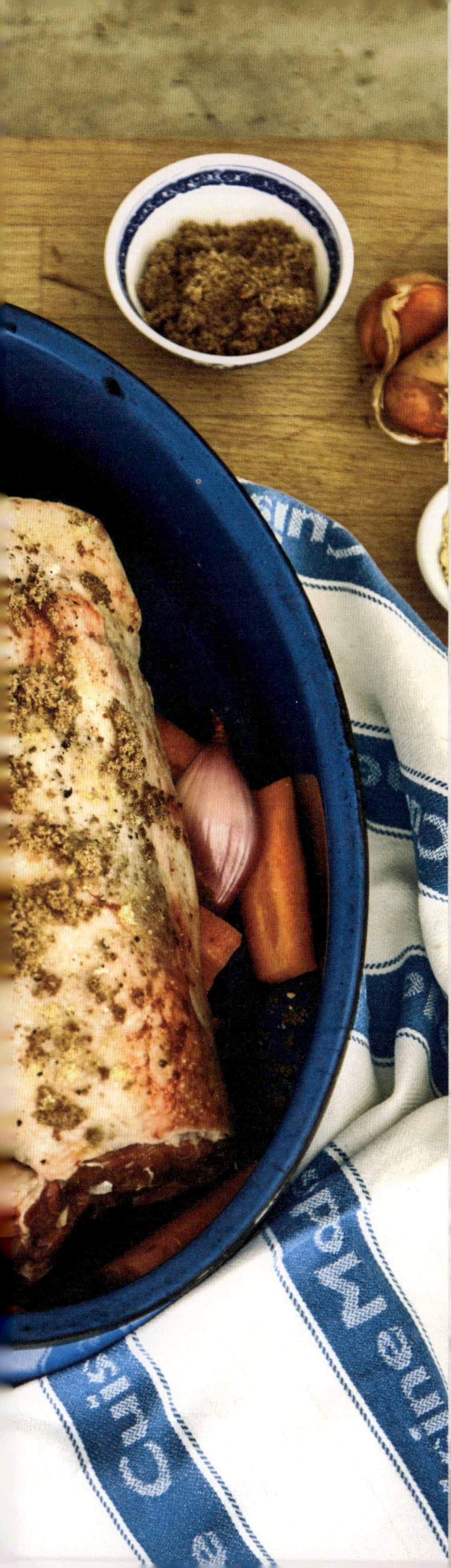

Roast potatoes
Parboil potatoes (until slightly cooked). Drain then shake the saucepan to roughen the edges and douse generously with olive oil, salt and pepper, adding unpeeled garlic and rosemary sprigs if you like. Tip into a separate baking dish and roast at 200°C (400°F, gas mark 6) for 1 hour till crisp and yummy.

TIP

Lamb fat sets very easily. Add ice cubes to slightly cooled jus and the fat will congeal on the cubes. Pour through a sieve and fat and ice remain, leaving pure jus.
This is a rich-flavoured dish and is nice served with a green vegetable or a simple green salad dressed with vinaigrette. Sometimes I add fresh mint leaves to the salad as a little reminder of old-fashioned mint sauce.

I have included this easy recipe - a delicious ricotta made from full-cream milk - as a tribute to the dairy cows in our area. My favourite is a locally produced full-fat brand that is extra creamy and even comes in old-fashioned glass bottles. Goat's milk can also be used.

Home-made ricotta

(serves 4-6)

Ingredients

- 2 litres full cream milk to make approx. 500g ricotta
- 1 teaspoon salt
- 2 teaspoons citric acid
- ¼ cup (60ml) water

Method

Add the salt to the milk in a stainless steel saucepan, stirring occasionally so it doesn't stick, and bring to near boiling (90–5°C/195°F). Remove from the heat.

Dissolve the citric acid in the water and add to the milk. It will curdle.

Leave the pan of milk on the bench until cool enough to handle.

Line a sieve with a scalded paper dishcloth or muslin cloth and pour in the curds. Leave to drain for 1–2 hours in the refrigerator. The ricotta is best used very fresh, but will last 2–3 days in the fridge.

The day before you intend to serve this dish, make the dressing and marinade the tomatoes. Use the best olives that you have available, and they can be kept whole so you can count 'Tinker, Tailor' with the stones once you've finished eating!

Fresh Ricotta with Tomatoes and Figs marinated in a Fennel Flavoured Dressing

(Serves 6-8)

Ingredients

500 g cherry tomatoes (or any ripe beautiful small tomatoes with stalks still attached)

1-2 fresh ripe black figs per person, halved

3-5 olives per person

fresh basil leaves

500g fresh ricotta made the day you wish to serve

Dressing

1 cup (240ml) olive oil

2 bay leaves

1 teaspoon chopped thyme

1 tablespoon chopped flat leaf parsley

1 garlic clove, peeled and halved

1 tablespoon of fennel seeds, crushed

1 tablespoon honey

⅓ cup (80ml) white balsamic vinegar

juice of ½ lemon

Method

Tomatoes

Score a crosscut in the base of each tomato.

Place them in a heatproof bowl and pour over boiling water to cover, count to 15, then using a slotted spoon, remove from water. Carefully peel away the skin, leaving the calyx and a little stalk intact. A snip here and there with scissors makes this easier. Set aside in a bowl and cover.

Dressing

In a small saucepan over a low heat, add the olive oil, chopped herbs, garlic and fennel seeds and barely simmer for 10 minutes. Remove from heat and add honey, balsamic vinegar and lemon juice. Season with salt and freshly ground pepper. Cool then pour over tomatoes and marinate overnight.

To Serve

Drain the tomatoes, reserving the marinade.

On a large platter, or individual plates, place a mound of fresh ricotta and then the tomatoes, figs and olives.

Whisk the marinade to emulsify and drizzle over the ricotta, figs and olives.

Garnish with a few torn basil leaves and serve with the best bread you can find.

TIP

I have successfully made this dish with dried figs which I have soaked in the marinade to plump and soften them and even substituted the ricotta with a store-bought soft feta when pressed for time.

This is my salute to summer and the tomato. I usually serve it as an entrée or as a lunch dish. It can also be cooked as one tart, in which case use a whole tomato for each slice. Black olives, pitted, look pretty between the tomatoes. You could delete the oil drizzle and serve with a green salad, including basil leaves.

There are five parts to this recipe: pre-baked tartelette shells (use greased fluted metal quiche dishes about 10cm/4in in diameter) a thick, jammy tomato sauce, soft goat's cheese, oven-roasted tomatoes, basil-flavoured oil.

Tartelettes of tomato and goat's cheese with a drizzle of basil-flavoured oil

(8 tartelettes or 1 x 27cm (10½ in) tart)

Ingredients

Pastry

1⅔ cup (200g) plain flour

large pinch salt

125g unsalted butter, chilled and cut into small pieces

approx. ⅓ cup (80ml) chilled water (approx. 6 tablespoons)

Method

Place the flour and salt in the bowl of a food processor and pulse to mix.

Add the butter pieces and pulse till butter is mixed into flour and looks like coarse damp sand.

Pulse the food processor while adding the water slowly, stopping as soon as the dough begins to clump together.

Turn on to a floured surface and form into a rectangular block. Rest for 1 hour at room temperature. Then roll out and line the greased tart tins, or use your fingers to press the pastry into the tins. Prick the bases with a fork.

Chill in the freezer for 30 mins. The tins could be stacked on top of one another, then placed in a fastened plastic bag in the fridge overnight.

Preheat oven to 220°C (425°F, gas mark 6–7).

Line the pastry with baking paper and weigh with rice and bake for 10–15 mins until the pastry edges are becoming golden. Take out of the oven, remove the paper and rice and return to the oven until the pastry is golden and cooked – about 5–10 mins.

Cool on a rack. Leave in the tins till serving time to protect the delicate pastry.

TIP

Divide the block of pastry evenly into 8 cubes and then roll thinly on a floured surface or pastry sheet. Press into tins with your fingers, then roll the rolling pin over the top to cut off any excess pastry (there will be very little, but what there is can be used to patch any thin sections). Home-made looks good; anyone can buy perfect tarts from a patisserie.

I make this dish often, ringing the changes with different accompaniments. I usually serve half a pear if having other things with it. A small wedge of a rich chocolate cake goes well, as does a rich good chocolate ice cream or even a small pot of old-fashioned *mousse au chocolat*. Vanilla ice-cream with a few curls of chocolate is simple and delicious.

Pears poached in a coffee syrup

Ingredients

half a firm dessert pear per person, peeled and halved lengthways - Beurre Blanc

2½ cups (600ml) strong black instant coffee, 2 teaspoons per cup

1 cup (225g) granulated sugar

Method

In a wide pan big enough to take the pears in one layer make a syrup with the sugar and the strong coffee, bringing to the boil and simmering for few minutes.

Reduce the heat till a tremble, and add the pears, rounded side down. The pears should be just covered in syrup. Add more coffee liquid if necessary.

Turn the pears carefully every now and then and finish with cut side down.

Simmer very gently until the pears start to become translucent around the edges and the tip of a knife penetrates very easily. Remove the pears with an egg slice to a shallow dish, rounded side up, and coat with a little of the syrup. Cover with cling film and refrigerate.

Return the syrup to the heat and bring to a rolling boil to thicken and reduce. Remember it will thicken as it cools. If by chance it is too thick when it cools add a little water and stir over a gentle heat.

Pour into a jug. Cool and chill.

Plate the pear and pour over a pool of syrup.

TIP:

Instant black coffee gives a better flavour in this dish than real coffee.
Serve this dish chilled for the best flavour. It can be made a day ahead of serving. For a pretty presentation, leave one half of each pear with the stalk intact, or with a sharp knife carefully cut the stalk in half lengthways. You can garnish the dish with roughly chopped walmuts.

A dish for autumn as the weather cools, the leaves turn and the field mushrooms appear. Although we live in the country, fresh, wild rabbit is not often available, and I use farmed rabbit for this dish. I cooked it as part of a 'Dirt road dinner' one autumn, inspired by the wild foods of autumn (chestnuts, walnuts, field mushrooms) and all things wild.
The semolina is a smoother, creamier version of polenta and cooks in minutes. While we wait for our truffle oaks to produce I find truffle oil is a good substitute.

Rabbit with field mushrooms and truffle-scented semolina

(serves 4–6)

Ingredients

- 4 tablespoons olive oil
- 2 rashers streaky bacon or pancetta, diced
- 1 large farmed rabbit, jointed into 6 good pieces
- 1 large onion, diced
- 12–18 small French shallots, peeled
- 12–18 button mushrooms
- 2 tablespoons flour
- salt and ground pepper
- 6 large open mushrooms, chopped small
- ½ bottle wine, red or white, or dry cider
- bouquet garni, tied with string between 2 celery sticks, bay leaf, lemon thyme, strip of lemon peel, parsley stalks
- 1–2 cloves garlic, peeled
- parsley, small bunch, chopped

Method

In a large wide casserole fry off the bacon in the olive oil until In a large wide casserole fry off the bacon in the olive oil until golden but still soft. Remove from the pan.

Add the washed and dried rabbit pieces to the pan and fry gently until golden in parts, turning them now and then. Remove from the pan.

Add the onions and shallots, adding more oil if necessary, and brown gently until golden. Add the button mushrooms and flour. Keep stirring and browning.

Season with salt and ground pepper, then remove from the pan.

Raise the heat a little and add the chopped mushrooms. Cook for a few minutes to soften and let the juices run.

Add a good slosh of wine, scrape up any sticky bits from the bottom of the pan and boil for a minute or two to evaporate the alcohol.

Return everything to the pan including any juice, the bouquet garni and garlic. Add a little water or more wine if it seems a little dry but do not drown your rabbit – the mushrooms will make more juice.

Simmer very gently for 50–60 mins.

If there is too much liquid remove the rabbit, onions and button mushrooms to a serving dish, cover and keep warm. Boil the liquid to reduce and concentrate the sauce to a glossy finish.

Taste and season. Pour over the rabbit, or return the rabbit to the pan and coat it with the sauce. Sprinkle with freshly chopped parsley.

TIP

Joint the rabbit into six pieces: four legs and two pieces from the saddle, plus some ribby bits for the pot. Remove the latter before serving. Trim excess bony bits from the legs if you like.

Tomato sauce

Ingredients

400g tin Italian tomatoes

1 onion, peeled and cut lengthwise into 8 pieces

clove garlic, peeled

2 tablespoons olive oil

Method

Empty the tomatoes into a saucepan with half a can of water.

Add the onion and garlic and several glugs of olive oil.

Simmer on the stove top until thick and almost jam-like, mashing occasionally with a potato masher.

Cool to room temperature and set aside, covered.

Taste. It may not need salt; canned tomatoes are often salty.

Oven-roasted tomatoes

Ingredients

red, ripe, firm, perfect even-sized tomatoes

thyme, sprigs

¼ cup olive oil and large pinch salt, mixed

black pepper

basil leaves, handful

Method

Thirty minutes in advance cut a 2cm slice from the stem end of each tomato to remove the hard core and place them on a rack to drain, cut side down.

Preheat the oven to 200°C (400°F, gas mark 6).

Brush a foil-lined baking tray with the salted oil.

Place the tomatoes on the tray, cut side down and brush with salted oil.

Sprinkle liberally with thyme sprigs and grind over pepper.

Bake for 20–30 mins until the skin begins to blister or split.

Set aside to cool to room temperature.

To assemble

Tartelettes are served at room temperature.

Place a pastry shell in the centre of each plate.

Spread some of the tomato sauce in the tart shell.

Place a spoonful of soft goat's cheese in the middle of the filled tart.

Carefully remove the skin from the roasted tomatoes, and with the help of an egg slice place a tomato half on top of the goat's cheese.

Brush with a little of the oil and tomato juices from the baking tray.

Process some basil to a purée, adding oil and juices from the tray (and extra oil if needed). Drizzle around the tartelette on each plate.

Any extra goat's cheese can be crumbled up and scattered on top.

Bon appétit!

TIP

Source the best-flavoured tomatoes money can buy, or showcase your home-grown beauties.

Spinach and ricotta gnocchi

(serves 4-6)

Ingredients

1 tablespoon onion, peeled and finely chopped

knob butter

750g wilted spinach, finely chopped (place in a pan with a smidge of water and cook briefly, or place in a colander and pour over a kettle of boiling water)

500g ricotta

1 pinch ground nutmeg

salt and pepper

3 eggs lightly beaten, plus 1 extra if necessary

2⁄3 cup (85g) plain flour

extra flour to dust

Method

Put on a large pot of salted water to boil.

Gently fry the onion in a little butter until soft but not coloured.

Wrap wilted spinach in an old clean tea towel and squeeze as hard as you can to remove excess liquid.

Combine the chopped spinach and onion (or whizz up in a food processor) then mix into the ricotta in a large bowl. Add nutmeg and season generously with salt and pepper.

Add the eggs and stir to combine. Gently mix in the flour. If the mixture seems dry add the extra beaten egg little by little.

Line an oven tray or similar with baking paper.

Dust additional plain flour onto an oven tray or on the bench (using a tray saves mess).

With floured hands roll about a tablespoon of mixture between your palms to make a small round.

Roll in a little extra flour, shake off the excess, then place the gnocchi on a paper-lined tray.

Test the first one in the simmering water. If it floats to the top and doesn't fall to bits there is enough flour in the mix – if it disintegrates add some more flour. Taste and adjust the seasoning if necessary (salt, pepper, nutmeg).

Cook in three batches, removing with a slotted spoon as the gnocchi rise to the surface.

TIP

The gnocchi can be eaten immediately with melted butter and Parmesan cheese, or any sauce you would serve with pasta. When dealing with large numbers I find it easier to put the gnocchi into a slightly buttered serving dish, pour over a nice tomato sauce and then sprinkle Parmesan cheese on top. The dish can be refrigerated until required then cooked in a moderate oven until hot and the cheese browns.

Pizza days are family days, or when we have a large group of friends to entertain casually. Pizza for two is not really practical as the wood-fired oven takes a long time to heat up: this recipe should produce enough pizza to feed a hungry family of five.

I usually make the dough and shape into rounds, ready to be pressed into trays, and have an assortment of toppings so everybody can have their own tailor-made pizza. You can decide how thick to leave the pizza crust – we like thin crusts in our family.

Pizza

(serves 5–6)

Ingredients

7½ cups (1kg) white bread flour or Italian Tipo'00' flour

or

6 cups (800g) strong white bread flour and 1 cup (200g) finely ground semolina flour

1 teaspoon fine sea salt

2 x 7g sachets dried yeast

1 tablespoon castor sugar

4 tablespoons olive oil

2¾ cups (650ml) lukewarm water

Method

Sift the flours and salt onto a clean bench or very large bowl and make a well in the middle.

Fill a jug with 650ml of warm water and add yeast, sugar and oil. Leave for a few minutes for the yeast to begin to work (froth) and pour into the well.

Using your finger tips drag the flour gradually into the well until all comes together into a ball. Knead until you have a springy ball.

Place the dough in a large flour-dusted bowl and flour the top of it. Cover the bowl with a damp clean tea towel and place in a warm spot for 1 hour until doubled in size.

Remove the dough to a flour-dusted surface and knead to knock out the air.

If using immediately divide the dough into 6–8 balls and roll or press out with fingers on to baking trays or pizza tins.

If making the dough before it is needed wrap the balls in cling film and refrigerate, bringing them back to room temperature before shaping.

Toppings

To make a basic tomato sauce lightly fry a peeled and finely chopped onion until soft, add a 400g can of diced tomatoes (imported Italian tomatoes are best) and cook gently until thick and unctuous. A splash of balsamic vinegar can be added at the end to give it a kick. Chilli, basil and herbs are optional extras.

Various cheeses: Parmesan, mozzarella, goat's cheese, blue vein etc.

Olives, anchovies, salami, prosciutto, pesto, rocket, artichokes ... and if kids are involved cheddar cheese, ham and pineapple pieces.

Leftover dough can be rolled by hand into 'snakes' for grissini.

TIP

My favourite is Pizza Bianca. Parboil a Desirée potato, and slice finely (using a mandoline ensures very fine slices – I leave the skin on). Toss in olive oil infused with a little garlic and sprigs of rosemary, salt and pepper, and arrange on the dough in a fishscale pattern. Scatter over a few rosemary leaves and drizzle with a little extra olive oil.

This dish is served twice a year when we pick our red Sangiovese grapes and when we process Shiraz grapes that we buy in. Buy the best thick, fatty, chunky, home-made-looking sausages you can find. Red table grapes could be substituted.

Pork and fennel sausages with red grape must

Ingredients

- as many sausages as pickers or guests
- a little plain flour
- 500ml red wine or grape juice per dozen sausages
- whole grapes, 2 large bunches
- salt and freshly ground pepper

Method

Brown the sausages in a pan deep enough to take the juice and grapes.

When a nice deep brown colour and nearly cooked remove the sausages from the pan and keep hot.

Add some flour to the pan juices and brown off, scraping up all the brown goodness from the bottom of the pan.

Add the wine or grape juice to the pan and stir to blend in the browned flour. Boil to reduce if necessary.

Return the sausages to the pan and add the whole grapes. Heat briefly. Taste and season.

Serve with a big mustardy green salad with finely sliced fennel, crusty bread and some local cheese to follow.

TIP

I serve the sausages, grapes and some of the sauce on a bed of wet polenta on a big deep platter and have a jug of extra sauce on the side. If there are small grandchildren present I usually cook ordinary snags and have a dish of macaroni cheese for those who only eat pasta.

We pick our olives when they are just beginning to colour. If we leave them any longer the birds try one, spit it out and try another, and on it goes. The original recipe was for Kalamata olives, but we have used this brine successfully with our assortment of varieties.

Easy brine-pickled olives

Ingredients

olives

125g cooking salt

1 litre water

1⅓ cups (330ml) malt vinegar

olive oil

Method

Pick over the olives carefully, rejecting badly bruised or pecked fruit.

Cover with water and soak overnight. If pressed for time you can soak longer, but if you do so change the water daily. If pressed for time you can soak longer, but if you do so change the water daily.

Pack the olives to near the top of clean glass jars.

Fill the jars with water (measure the amount so that you will know how much brine will be needed to cover the olives). Drain off the water.

Make up the brine in the proportions given above and pour over the olives. Do not add any flavourings at this stage (see Tip Box).

Top with olive oil to cover.

Seal the jars, either with screw tops or clip tops with rubber seals and put them in a dark cupboard and forget about them for six months. Taste, and leave longer if the olives are still bitter. They will keep for some years.

TIP

A flavourless cooking oil may be used instead of olive oil. Do not be tempted to use wine vinegar in the brine as it will ferment. Flavourings such as garlic, herbs, citrus peel and so on can be added a few days before eating. Only add flavouring to jars that you will consume within a few weeks.

You can actually soak the olives for a couple of days. Just ensure that you change the water daily.

This simple, quickly cooked dish of softly sautéd onion and zucchini with paprika-spiked cream complements a crispy roasted chicken beautifully. I make this dish frequently in summer when zucchinis are plentiful. I choose Gippsland cream because it is thick enough to hold up a spoon and is produced by cows which graze on some of the greenest grass in Australia which I can see from my kitchen. Of course if you are not fortunate enough to have access to Gippsland pure cream, any good thick cream may be substituted.

Zucchini paprika and cream

(serves 4)

Ingredients

knob butter

1 small onion, peeled and finely chopped

2 small to medium zucchini, washed but not peeled, cut into 6cm batons

1-2 tablespoons sweet paprika (or to taste)

salt and a little ground pepper

1-2 tablespoons thick Gippsland pure cream, 45% butterfat

A good handful of fresh parsley leaves

Method

Gently sweat the onion in the butter until soft but not brown.

Add the zucchini batons, salt, pepper and paprika and toss.

Increase the heat and continue until cooked but still with some 'bite'.

If a lot of liquid forms boil briefly to reduce.

Add cream and parsley, and stir the mixture to coat the zucchini.

TIP

This also goes nicely with pork fillet.
If you are like me and buy a punnet of zucchini seedlings and cannot resist planting all of them you will have enough flowers to contemplate stuffing them. A peeled, preferably raw prawn makes a simple and delicious filling. Dust the prawn in a little plain flour, squeeze it closed and briefly shallow fry in olive oil until crisp. Eat immediately!

MUNDIAL

A robust salad which can be served as a standalone dish. The cooked vinegar, bacon fat and olive oil makes a tangy dressing. The quantities given below are for one person; adjust the quantities to suit the number of guests.

Warm salad of silver beet with bacon lardons and pinenuts

(serves 1)

Ingredients

large handful of young silver beet leaves, well washed, large ribs removed and torn into bite-size pieces

olive oil

pinenuts

half a rasher of streaky bacon cut into lardons (with some fat)

black pepper

red wine or balsamic vinegar

Method

Place the torn silver beet leaves in a heatproof ceramic serving bowl.

Toast the pinenuts in a little oil in a frying pan then remove.

Add the lardons to the oil, fry until crisp (being careful not to burn the oil and bacon fat) and scatter over the silver beet.

Add a little more oil to the pan, if necessary, and add coarsely ground black pepper

While the pan is still hot add a good slosh of red wine or vinegar and stir up any crusty bacon bits remaining.

While still boiling pour this dressing over the prepared silver beet and bacon mixture and toss. The silver beet will wilt a little. Scatter over the toasted pinenuts and serve immediately.

TIP

When toasting the pinenuts don't take your eyes off them - they burn easily.
And a warning to note before you add the wine or vinegar to the hot pan: the fumes can take your breath away, so avert your face.

This is a version of a cabbage salad that I have been making for years. When we lived in Perth in the late 1960s we often ate in a Hungarian restaurant in Northbridge. What kept us returning was a cabbage salad that accompanied nearly every dish on the menu. Mine is still not as good as theirs but it is a long way to go for a cabbage fix. I now have a basic version which changes countries when I change the flavourings.

Cabbage salad

(serves 6–8)

Ingredients for the Hungarian original

¼ large cabbage, sliced as finely as possible

½ white salad onion, grated

1 small cucumber, peeled in stripes, seeds scraped out and coarsely grated

½ green capsicum, grated (see Tip Box)

olive oil

white cider vinegar

ground black pepper and salt

Method

Place the cabbage in a large bowl. Salt it well and let it stand for a while to soften. Pour off any liquid that may form.

Add the onion, cucumber and capsicum and toss well.

Add a few glugs of olive oil and a slosh of white cider vinegar, ground pepper and taste for salt

TIP

To successfully grate a capsicum cut it in half, then trim each half so that you have two flat pieces. Hold the inner flesh side against the grater with the flat of your fingers and grate until only the skin is left.

Cucumber can be grated the same way if you do not care for the skin.

Vietnamese version

(serves 6–8)

Ingredients

½ long Chinese cabbage, finely sliced crosswise then into 4cm lengths

¼ white salad onion, grated, or spring onions, sliced finely length-wise and into 4cm batons

1 small cucumber, peeled in stripes, seeds scraped out and coarsely grated

½ green capsicum, grated (see Tip Box)

coriander, bunch, chopped

Vietnamese mint, bunch, chopped

red chilli, finely sliced

sesame seeds, toasted

Dressing

4 tablespoons olive oil

2–4 tablespoons fish sauce

2 tablespoons red wine vinegar

2 tablespoons fresh lime juice

few drops sesame oil

grated palm sugar (or sugar) to taste

1 clove garlic, crushed with blade of a knife

Whisk all the ingredients together. Taste and adjust flavours to suit.

Add to the cabbage mix and toss. Sprinkle over toasted sesame seeds.

Our local butcher specialises in rare-breed, free-range pork and this is one of our favourite ways of cooking his lovely product.

Crisp pork belly cooked in pear or apple cider

(serves 4–6)

Ingredients

approx. 2kg slab of boned belly pork, scored

salt and ground pepper

1 tablespoon white vinegar

1 onion, sliced

1–3 whole star anise (pear version)

1–3 whole cloves (apple cider version)

2–2½ cups (500–625ml) of pear or apple cider (750ml bottle)

pears, cored, unpeeled and quartered (2 per person)

or

small cooking apples, small, cored, unpeeled and quartered (2 per person)

Method

Remove any wrapping from the pork and store it uncovered in the fridge to dry the skin.

Preheat the oven to 240–250°C (450–500°F, gas mark 9).

Season the flesh side of the pork well with salt and pepper.

Brush the skin with the vinegar and rub salt generously into skin, to help produce crackling.

In a heavy cast iron baking dish (not much bigger than the piece of pork) place the sliced onion and the star anise/cloves. Then place the pork, skin side up, on top.

Roast for about 30 mins at the high temperature until the skin starts to crackle. Sometimes it seems to take longer, but keep an eye on it as you don't want it to burn.

Reduce the heat to 180°C (350°F, gas mark 4) and pour the cider around the pork to about halfway up the sides

Cook for a further 1½ hours, turning the oven lower if the pork seems to be browning too much. Sometimes, despite all tricks, the skin refuses to crackle. Place it under a griller but do not leave it for a second – the crackling happens very quickly and can burn easily. My family get very cross if the crackling is burnt.

Remove from the baking dish and put aside to rest.

Pear or apple garnish

Place the quartered pears/apples in the baking dish while the pork is resting and roast for approx. 20–30 mins until they feel soft when poked with the tip of a knife .The pears will cook more quickly than the apples. Set aside and keep warm.

Sauce

Remove the star anise/cloves and put the baking dish over a low heat, scraping the onion and brown bits up from the bottom, and add more cider to make a sauce. Reduce if necessary. Taste. Sometimes a little sugar is called for, depending on the cider, or in reverse a dash of balsamic if it seems too sweet.

Ask the butcher to score the skin of the pork, taking into account portion sizes.

TIP

I serve the pear version with a Vietnamese-inspired salad of Chinese cabbage, and the apples with a Hungarian-inspired cabbage salad.

This is a cake for people who can't or don't usually make cakes: a one-step beautifully moist cake made in the food processor.

Easy peasy orange cake

(8–12 slices)

Ingredients

180g melted butter or soft margarine

1 whole orange roughly chopped into smallish pieces (remove the hard bit where the stem joined)

1½ cups (185g) self-raising flour

1 cup (220g) caster sugar

3 eggs

Method

Preheat oven to 180°C (350°F, gas mark 4).

Melt the butter in a cup in the oven while it is heating.

Grease and line a 23cm (9in) springform tin.

Place the orange (pips and skin included) in the food processor and process till mushy.

Add the flour, sugar, eggs and melted butter and process till just combined.

Pour into the lined tin and smooth the surface. Bake for 45–50 mins.

Cool in the tin for a few minutes before releasing the springform.

Dust with icing sugar – and enjoy!

TIP

I serve this cake simply dusted with icing sugar, but orange icing is nice. For a retro 'Jaffa' effect you could drizzle it with melted chocolate or ice with chocolate ganache.
If given a chance, it keeps well.

I make this cake whenever we gather to bottle last year's wine or pick the current season's grapes. It is moist, light and delicious, and best served warm from the oven.

Grapepickers' cake

(serves 8)

Ingredients

2 large eggs, at room temperature

⅔ cup (150g) caster sugar

4 tablespoons olive oil

60g melted butter, cooled

5 tablespoons milk

½ teaspoon vanilla essence

1⅔ cup (200g) plain flour

¾ teaspoon baking powder

pinch salt

grated zest of 1 lemon and 1 orange

300g red wine grapes (red table grapes are acceptable)

Method

Preheat the oven to 180°C (350°F, gas mark 4).

Generously butter and flour a 23cm (9in) springform tin.

With an electric beater whisk the eggs and sugar for approx. 3 mins until thick and lemon coloured.

Add oil, butter, milk and vanilla and mix to blend.

Sift flour, baking powder and salt into another bowl. Add the grated zests and toss to coat with the flour mixture.

Add this to the egg mixture and stir with a wooden spoon until thoroughly blended. Stand for 10 mins.

Stir about three-quarters of the grapes into the mixture. Pour into the prepared tin and smooth the top with a spatula.

Bake for 15 mins then scatter the remaining grapes over the top and bake for about another 40 mins till golden brown and firm to the touch.

Rest for at least 10 mins on a wire rack.

Serve straight from the tin, and if using a springform tin leave on the base.

Dust with icing sugar, stand back and wait for compliments!

TIP

For a bigger, shallower cake (more slices) a 30cm (12in) paella pan works well. (Note that if you have used the wider tin the overall cooking time may be reduced.)

A simple stove-top dish made with fresh spring vegetables from the garden (though frozen peas work equally well). I grow a perennial onion or tree onion which has both shallot-like onions at the bottom and, on the stem, little bulblets. These are like the tiny, luridly coloured cocktail onions, preserved in vicious vinegar, that were de rigueur on toothpicks with a cube of processed cheese in the 1970s. Perfect for this dish too!

Chicken with braised peas and baby onions

Ingredients

4-6 free-range chicken drumsticks and thighs (in one piece)

salt and pepper

1-2 tablespoons of olive oil

small nob of butter

lemon thyme, sprigs

1 clove garlic, unpeeled and squashed

20g butter

½-⅔ cup (150ml) water

Method

With strong kitchen scissors divide the drumstick and thigh. Trim off the knuckle from the drumstick (for aesthetic reasons) and remove any excess fat. Season with salt and pepper.

In a wide heavy-based pan heat the oil and butter together then brown the chicken pieces till a rich golden brown.

Add the lemon thyme sprigs, garlic, butter and water. Reduce the heat, and with the lid askew cook gently for 30–40 mins until tender. There should be a small quantity of cooking juices remaining, just enough to glaze the finished dish.

Braised peas and onions

Ingredients

5 small French shallots per person

25g butter

lemon thyme, sprigs

500g peas, thawed if frozen

½-⅔ cup (150ml water)

salt and pepper to taste

2 small heads of cos lettuce, shredded

Method

About 15 mins before the chicken is ready toss the onions in the butter and cook gently, stirring now and again for 8–10 mins.

Add the thyme, peas and water and cook gently for 5–6 mins till tender and water has almost disappeared (if using fresh peas this may take a little longer). Taste and season.

Add the lettuce, stir and cook until wilted (about a minute).

Spread the braised peas and onions on a platter (or individual plates) and arrange the chicken pieces on top. Glaze with the remaining jus. Tiny new potatoes, boiled and buttered go well with this fresh-tasting dish.

TIP

A mélange of spring vegetables can be cooked in the same way. Sometimes in early spring there may be just a few vegetables ready to eat at one time. For instance a handful of broad beans and peas, tiny little artichokes (sometimes it is best to pick the first artichoke early so as to bring the side shoots on), wee potatoes, leeks, Dutch carrots and so on – and you can always add a bit of pancetta to make a delicious savoury dish.

One of the citrus trees in our orchard is a tangelo, a cross between a tangerine and a grapefruit. I never knew what to do with the fruit as it is not really a fresh eating variety and there is a limit to how much marmalade a family can eat. As so often, Maggie Beer inspired me with a recipe for a tangelo flavoured crème brûlée. With eggs from our mademoiselles and fruit from our citrus grove this is a rich and unctuous dish to end a meal with. A small salad of citrus - segments or slices of tangelo, blood orange, pink or ruby grapefruit - make a nice accompaniment. To gild the lily, serve with a citrus flavoured madeleine.

Burnt tangelo cream

The quantity below serves 6-8 in 60ml custard cups. Double the recipe for a 1-litre bowl to serve 12.

(serves 6-8)

Ingredients

3 tangelos (or enough to make 250ml juice, or use fresh orange juice)

¼ cup (60g) golden caster sugar

300ml pouring cream (35% butterfat)

1 x 55g free range whole egg

2 x 55g free range egg yolks

Method

Preheat oven to 180°C (350°F, gas mark 4) if using a large bowl; turn it down a notch to 170°C (325–350°F, gas mark 3–4) for small cups.

Remove the zest in a long strip from two tangelos.

Juice all three (the required amount of liquid can be made up with orange juice).

Bring the juice, zest and caster sugar to boil in an enamelled or stainless steel saucepan, stirring to dissolve the sugar.

Boil until the syrup becomes a deep amber colour. Remove the strips of zest. Stir in the cream and remove from the heat.

Whisk the egg and yolks in a bowl, then whisk in the tangelo caramel.

Strain through a fine sieve into your chosen serving dishes.

Place the bowl or cups in a baking dish lined with a tea towel to stop them sliding as you put them in the oven.

Place the baking dish in the oven and carefully pour hot water around the containers to come two thirds of the way up the sides.

Bake for 45 mins (large bowl) and check after 30 mins for the smaller dishes. The cream will set with a slight crust.

Remove the serving dishes from the water-filled baking dish and allow to cool completely (see Tip Box) before covering with cling wrap and refrigerating.

TIP

Substitute oranges if tangelos are not available. Refrigerating while hot causes condensation to form on the cling wrap which spoils the look of the cream. Small pots of cream are easier to serve elegantly than spooning perfect quenelles of cream onto a plate.

Little demi-tasse-sized coffee cups can be used instead of custard cups or any small heatproof ramekin. Measure the volume of the cups and adjust the recipe to suit.

A hearty soup using all the last of the summer vegetable crop and the first pumpkin. Pistou is a tasty cold sauce from Provence, similar to Italian Pesto that is stirred into the soup. The vegetables should be diced into approx. 15mm pieces.

Autumn Soup with Basil Pistou

(serves 6)

Ingredients

2 tablespoons olive oil

2 brown onions, peeled and diced

2 medium carrots, diced

2 sticks of celery, diced

1 large potato (approx. 300g), peeled and diced

a piece of pumpkin (approx. 400-500g before peeling), roughly diced

1-2 cloves garlic, peeled and chopped

500g tomatoes, blanched, peeled and diced

250g vine-dried beans, precooked in water for 30 minutes

1 small zucchini, diced

3-4 leaves of kale, sliced and chopped

125g macaroni

Pistou

bunch of basil, leaves picked

coarse salt and freshly ground pepper

6 small cloves of garlic, peeled

100g freshly grated Parmesan cheese

½ cup (120ml) olive oil

Method for soup

In a large saucepan, gently heat the olive oil and sweat the onion, carrots, celery, potato, pumpkin, garlic and tomatoes, adding them to the pan as you prepare them until softened. Add the precooked beans

Add 4 litres of boiling water and simmer gently for about 45 minutes until the vegetables are soft.

Add the zucchini, kale and pasta and cook for a further 20 minutes.

Method for Pistou

In a food processor, or mortar and pestle if you prefer, process or pound the basil leaves and coarse salt, pepper and garlic to a coarse puree. Add some Parmesan and then loosen with some olive oil. Continue until all ingredients are thoroughly mixed.

Serve the pistou in a small bowl for people to add it to the soup to taste.

TIP

As we grow purple podded beans (the dried beans are white), this is what I tend to use for this soup, but any bean which has dried on the vine is fine. Of course, store-bought dried white haricot beans can be used if soaked overnight before precooking, or, at a pinch a can of white beans will do.

Our quince trees are prolific but despite the hardness of the fruit, birds seem to be able to damage them. I make the jelly often from windfalls, cutting out the brown and pecked bits! Quinces are very high in pectin so usually there is no problem with setting.
You will need a jelly bag or large square of cheese cloth or similar to drip the jelly through. I use an old piece of terylene curtain which I keep for the purpose.

Quince Jelly and Conserve

Ingredients

quinces
water
white sugar

Method

Wash the furry bloom from the quinces.

Do not peel but trim off any brown bits and roughly chop with a heavy cook's knife, approximately into eighths. Do not core.

Place the quinces in a large, deep pan and barely cover with cold water.

Bring to a slow simmer and cook gently until very soft and until the quince have turned a rich brick red colour, which is usually between 1 and 2 hours. The longer the cooking time the better the finished colour will be.

Place a large sieve or colander over a large basin or preserving pan. Line the sieve/colander with the cheesecloth and carefully pour the quince and water into it. Without squeezing the contents, tie the ends of the cloth as if tying up a swag and then tie with string to make it secure. Your swag should now be a loose ball shape similar to a Christmas pudding. This 'pudding' of quince now has to be suspended so the juice drips through the cloth and into the deep basin or preserving pan. If the preserving pan is sufficiently deep the quince bundle can hang from a wooden spoon placed across the top of the pan. The bottom of the bundle should not touch the dripped liquid. (I rig up a contraption using a loose bottomed kitchen chair with a basin underneath.)

Let the fruit drip overnight. DO NOT SQUEEZE the jelly swag as this will make the finished product cloudy.

Wrap the swag of pulp in clingwrap and set aside in the fridge.

The next day

Measure the liquid by cups and then measure out equal cups of sugar. (Warming the sugar in the oven helps it dissolve quicker.)

In a deep pan bring the juice and sugar to the boil, stirring until all the sugar is dissolved, then bring to a rolling boil. Skim the froth from the surface as necessary. Boil for approx. 20 minutes.

While the jelly is boiling, place a couple of saucers in the fridge, and wash and warm jars to sterilise them. I put them through the fast cycle in the dishwasher.

To test for setting point place a little of the hot jelly mixture on a cold saucer, leave for a minute then push your finger through the cooled jelly. The jelly should not run and the surface should wrinkle, setting as it cools.

Place your jars on a heatproof surface – such as a large wooden chopping board – and carefully ladle the hot jelly into the sterilised jars filling nearly to the top, because the jelly shrinks as it cools. A wide neck funnel makes this easier and safer.

Seal the jars while hot.

Quince Conserve for the Cheeseboard

With the remaining pulp a thick jam can be made if you have a large Moulinex sieve left over from pre-foodprocessor days. A long handled, sturdy wooden spoon and gloves are also necessary

Tip the swag of pulp, seeds and skin into the mouli and push it through. Alternatively, you can use a wooden spoon to push the pulp through a sieve if you're patient and strong! The resulting puree will be thick and a little grainy.

Measure the puree, then add 1 cup sugar to each cup of puree.

In a thick-bottomed pan gently heat the puree and sugar, stirring continuously. Do not let the mixture boil until sugar is completely dissolved.

As the mixture boils it will spit and plop like a hot mud pool, so take care.

Stir continuously to prevent burning and sticking, until the jam begins to come away from the sides of the pan, approximately 15 minutes.

Spoon into wide necked, sterilised jars while hot and seal.

After all this palaver I like to sit the finished jars of carnelian coloured jelly and conserve on the kitchen table for a few days to be admired.

This piquant salad originates from the Auvergne mountains in Central France where Salers cheese is produced. Cream is used instead of oil.

Cheesemaker's mignonette salad

(serves 6)

Ingredients

2 small French shallots, peeled and sliced, separated into fine rings

1 tablespoon red wine vinegar

2–3 tablespoons thick cream

salt and pepper to taste

1 soft lettuce

Method

Steep thinly sliced rings of French shallot in some red wine vinegar to soften for at least 15 mins (and up to 4 hours).

At serving time add thick cream to the shallot mixture until it reaches a dressing consistency, and season with salt and pepper.

Wash and dry any soft lettuce variety, i.e. butter, mignonette, and toss gently in the dressing.

TIP

This is particularly good with a simple grilled steak or rare roasted hot or cold beef.

Unfortunately our truffle oaks have so far proved to be barren so this dish is flavoured with truffle oil.

Creamy truffle-scented semolina

(serves 6–8)

Ingredients

1 litre full cream milk

1 bayleaf (optional)

2 teaspoons salt

1 cup (170g) fine white semolina

1 teaspoon truffle oil

or

60g grated Parmesan cheese

Method

Bring the milk to a gentle simmer in an enamelled or stainless steel saucepan over a moderate heat.

Add the salt.

In a slow steady stream, while stirring with a wooden spoon, add the semolina.

Stir for 3–5 mins and it will form a creamy mass.

Add the truffle oil or Parmesan and mix well. Taste for seasoning, and serve.

TIP

You could infuse the milk with a bayleaf if you wish, but remember to remove it before adding the salt.

Parmesan cheese may be substituted for the truffle oil if the scent of truffle is not your cup of tea.

Broccoli or cauliflower dressed with an anchovy sauce

(serves 6)

Ingredients

large head of broccoli or 1 small cauliflower, broken into florets

1 small can (approx. 45g) flat anchovies, in oil

1 clove garlic, finely chopped or smashed with the back of a cook's knife

olive oil

dry coarse breadcrumbs

coarsely ground black pepper

Method

Cook the broccoli or cauliflower in boiling water until only just done. Drain (retain some of the cooking water if planning on serving with pasta – see Tip Box).

Crisp the breadcrumbs in a pan in a smidge of olive oil. Set aside.

In a saucepan (use a large one if serving with pasta), add the anchovies (and their oil), a few good splashes of olive oil and the garlic. Cook gently, taking care that the garlic doesn't burn, until the anchovies melt into a sauce.

Add the broccoli or cauliflower to the sauce and toss to coat, then add crisp breadcrumbs and toss gently again. Taste. It may not need salt but black pepper is essential.

TIP

This is delicious when served with orecchiette pasta. Add the cooked pasta to the sauce in the saucepan, toss, adding the reserved cooking water to moisten if needed.
It also makes a great vegetable dish in its own right.

Crostata is a cross between a cake and a pastry. It makes an easy rustic dessert, or a cake to have with coffee at any time.
The fillings are only limited by your imagination, and I have tried raspberry jam (made by my friend), sweet orange marmalade, apricot jam, rhubarb chopped finely with a few strawberries and sugar, cooked apple and fresh blackberry, poached quince, honey mixed with slivered almonds, sliced stone fruit and more!

Crostata

(serves 8+)

Ingredients

2½ cups (300g) plain flour

⅔ cup (150g) sugar (caster or granulated)

150g butter, melted

2 large eggs, beaten

pinch of salt

2 scant teaspoons baking powder

filling of your choice (see Tip Box)

Method

In a bowl, with a wooden spoon, mix flour, sugar, melted butter, beaten eggs, salt and baking powder into a soft biscuit-like dough.

Form the dough into a ball and rest for 30 mins in the refrigerator.

Preheat oven to 180°C (350°F, gas mark 4).

Grease with butter a 23cm (9in) round pie dish, approximately 5cm (2½in) deep, or shallow cake tin.

When the dough has rested cut off a one third piece and put aside in the frig.

Press the rest of the dough into the dish or tin, evenly, with your fingers, pressing up the sides to form a shallow well in the middle with a thickish wall.

Place your chosen filling on the dough, spreading evenly.

On a sheet of baking paper roll out the remaining dough quite thickly and cut it into strips about 3cm (1½in) wide.

With the help of a wide-bladed knife place the strips on top of the filling in a criss-cross (lattice) pattern.

The dough is very soft and biscuit-like and may break in places, but just patch it up and it will look fine when cooked.

Cook in the oven for 30 mins. It will be puffed up and very handsome.

Dust with icing sugar.

TIP

When you fill the pie dish make sure you have enough filling to reach to the top of the pastry wall. If you are using raw rhubarb mound the filling a little higher.
This cake/pastry is rich and small slices only are needed with a cup of coffee.
For a dessert, pouring cream in a pretty jug is a nice accompaniment.

When we make our white wine, Pinot Gris, we try to begin picking early in the morning while the temperature is low, so as to preserve the freshness in the grapes and therefore the wine. To guarantee 'early starters' to pick we have a dinner the night before. A quail farm nearby produces these delicious little birds, and the other ingredients are only a step away.

Quails dressed in prosciutto with Pinot Gris grapes

Ingredients

1-2 quail each, depending on size (and what you serve with them)

handful of grapes per person

2 fresh vine leaves per bird

salt and pepper

1 small clove of garlic per bird, plus extra

lemon thyme, bunch

butter, softened

1 slice prosciutto per bird

Pinot Gris wine

thick cream (45 per cent butterfat)

Method

Preheat the oven to 200°C (400°F, gas mark 6).

Wash the quails under cold running water and dry thoroughly.

Wash and dry grapes and vine leaves.

Rub salt and pepper generously inside each bird.

Stuff each quail with a few grapes, a small quorm of garlic and a sprig of thyme, and rub with the softened butter.

Wrap a slice of prosciutto around each quail. Sit it on a vine leaf and place another leaf on top. To secure the prosciutto and vine leaves to each bird, cut a longish piece of kitchen twine and tie the quail's legs together, leaving two ends of equal-length twine. Truss the quail by wrapping each length of twine around the bird in order to secure the leaves and prosciutto by tying the lengths together. Butter a heavy roasting dish generously and place the quails in the dish, breast side up, leaving room between them for the grapes.

Poke small unpeeled or halved cloves of garlic here and there to taste among the quail and roast for 15 mins.

Add a handful of grapes per person to the dish and roast for another 15 mins. Check that the grapes remain moist. Add a splash of wine if dry.

Test the quail are cooked by wiggling a leg: it should move freely. When ready place the birds on a serving dish and keep warm.

Place the baking dish with the grapes on a gentle heat and scrape up any golden goodness from the bottom of the dish. Add some wine and a little water and bring to the boil to make a sauce. Reduce a little and add a few spoonfuls of thick cream to finish. Taste and season with salt and pepper if necessary, then pour over the quail.

TIP

Omit the vine leaves if they are not available. Sometimes I place each quail on a slice of sourdough bread which I have buttered and crisped in the oven. Potatoes boulangères- a sliced potato and onion bake, made with chicken stock rather than cream - accompany this dish beautifully.

Freshly dug Kiphler potatoes are perfect for potato salad. When sliced the skins peel very easily and the size is just right.
I originally found this recipe (which I have been making for years) in an old French cookbook.

French style potato salad

(serves 6-8)

Ingredients

For 1kg potatoes (8-9 medium size)

4 tablespoons dry white wine

2 tablespoons chicken stock (can be made with cubes)

2 tablespoons white cider vinegar

splodge Dijon mustard

6 tablespoons olive oil

salt and pepper

finely chopped spring onion or chives, parsley etc.

Method

Boil the potatoes in their skins until just cooked. When cool slice and peel.

Pour the wine and chicken stock over the warm potatoes. Set aside until absorbed.

Whisk together vinegar, mustard, salt and olive oil in the serving bowl. Season to taste (remembering that potatoes really love salt!).

Add the chopped herbs and gently toss together to mix.

Can be served warm or chilled. A little extra dressing may be needed if the salad stands long before serving.

TIP

Various additions can be added to the base dish, such as a little cream with paprika and walnuts, cream, mashed anchovies and finely sliced spring onions, green beans, red onion and hard-boiled egg.

I like this recipe because the peapods are used. I hate tossing the pods to the chooks after all that effort of shelling.
My particular risotto method is simpler than usual: 20 mins covered cooking then 5 mins stirring.
There are four steps to this recipe: peapod stock, pea purée, risotto, and a little garnish of crisp proscuitto or bacon.

Garden pea risotto

Ingredients and method for peapod stock

1kg fresh peas in the pod, shelled, peas put to one side

3 cups icy water

Blanch 350g of fresh peapods (after shelling) in a pot of boiling water. Drain.

Plunge the pods into a bowl containing 1½ cups of icy cold water to set the colour.

Process the pods with the water. Strain through a fine sieve or mouli, discard the fibrous bits and set aside the pea stock.

Reserve ¼ cup of stock for the pea purée and 2 cups for the risotto – make up the amount with water if you don't have quite enough.

pea purée

Ingredients and method for pea purée

100g peas

knob butter

¼ cup (60ml) pea stock

Method
Cook gently in a saucepan for about 5 mins, then process till smooth.

risotto

(serves 4)
Ingredients for risotto

½ onion, peeled and finely chopped

1 small clove garlic, finely chopped and smashed

2 tablespoons butter

1¼ cups (200g) Arborio or Italian Carnaroli rice

⅓ cup (80ml) white wine

2 cups reserved pea stock

salt and pepper

Parmesan cheese to taste

1 slice proscuitto or bacon

Method
Gently fry the onion and garlic in the butter till transluscent.

Add the rice and cook gently, stirring, until rice is shiny (4–5 mins).

Pour in the white wine and pea stock. Add salt and pepper. Stir then cover and cook very gently for 20 mins. Occasionally check that it is not cooking too fast.

After 20 mins stir for another 5 mins, then stir in the pea purée and Parmesan cheese.

Taste and season with salt and pepper. A little lemon juice or white wine can be added to sharpen the flavour.

While the risotto is cooking gently fry some small dice of proscuitto or lardons of bacon until crisp.

Serve the risotto in shallow bowls, topped with the prosciutto or bacon and a shaving of Parmesan.

TIP

The best thing about this recipe is that by cooking very gently you avoid having to tediously stir while adding the liquid little by little. An induction cooktop which controls the heat would be foolproof, but I manage on my wood-fired stove. On gas, which sometimes is hard to regulate to a slow, slow simmer, a simmer mat could be useful.

A different way of presenting an old favourite. Fiddly perhaps, but fun - and very pretty. Each of the elements - meringue, rose syrup, raspberry sauce, crystallised rose petals and buds and strawberry garnish - are simple, the most difficult being removing the paper coll.

Pavlova 'en pointe'

(serves 6)

Ingredients

6 squares non-stick baking paper, 20 x 20cm (7¾ x 7¾in)

Paper clips

Meringue

4 egg whites

1⅛ cup (250g) caster sugar

2 teaspoons cornflour

1 teaspoon vinegar

1 teaspoon vanilla extract

Rose syrup

1 cup (220g) sugar

1 cup (250ml) water

1 tablespoon rosewater

1 small handful perfumed rose petals, preferably home grown; if using florist's roses wash well

Raspberry sauce

1 punnet raspberries

2 tablespoons caster sugar

lemon juice to taste

Method

Preheat oven to 120°C (250°F, gas mark 1).

Fold each square of baking paper in half to make a strip measuring 10 x 20cm (4 x 7¾in). Join the ends together (overlapping slightly) to make a ring, and secure with paper clips.

Place on a baking-paper-lined oven tray.

Meringue

Beat the egg whites till they begin to hold their shape. Add the sugar in four parts, roughly 3 mins apart, beating well at high speed until stiff and glossy.

Sift over the cornflour, then add the vinegar and vanilla and mix in at a low speed.

Pipe or spoon the meringue into the paper collars.

Cook for 1 hour. Turn off the oven and leave the pavlovas to cool for 30 mins.

Rose syrup

Combine the caster sugar, water, rosewater and petals. Simmer for 5–10 mins, cool and strain. Reserve the syrup.

Raspberry sauce

In a small saucepan crush the raspberries, add the sugar and simmer for a few minutes. Cool and sieve. Add lemon juice to taste.

Crystallised rose petals and 'Cecile Brunner' buds

24-36 small pink or red rose petals

12-18 tiny rosebuds, washed gently and dried

1 egg white

½ cup (110g) caster sugar

Garnish to serve

1 punnet strawberries, small to medium size fruit

300ml whipped cream

Crystallised petals and buds

Whisk the egg white a little to loosen. Hold each petal or bud with tweezers and, using an artist's paintbrush, coat with egg white. Dredge with sugar over a paper-lined tray, turning each petal to coat it evenly. Set on the tray to dry, then store in an airtight container.

Garnish

Whip the cream until it holds its shape and slice the strawberries lengthwise into pointed 'ballet slipper' shapes.

To assemble

Lay out six dessert plates. Carefully place one meringue in the middle of each plate and remove the paper collars, either by snipping the paper with scissors or removing the clips.

Top each one with a generous dollop of cream, then arrange the strawberries (pointed ends up) on top of the cream.

Drizzle the strawberries and the plate with a little syrup and the raspberry sauce.

Finally place the crystallised petals between the strawberries, scatter the buds on the plate ... and take a bow.

TIP

The rose petal syrup, raspberry sauce and crystallised petals and buds may be prepared the day before. The meringue is best done the day it is to be served. It has a soft marshmallow texture with a crisp outer case.

If you are lucky enough to have in your garden 'Madame Isaac Pereire' her petals are perfect for the rose syrup, but any perfumed rose is fine

A family favourite! We serve it with roast lamb, pork or beef, and it is lovely with duck.

Braised red cabbage with apple

(serves 4–6)

Ingredients

A splash of olive oil

1 small onion, peeled, halved and sliced finely

1 clove garlic, chopped

1 apple, peeled, quartered and sliced

¼ red cabbage, sliced

2 cloves

splash of red wine, cider or balsamic vinegar

salt and pepper to taste

Method

In a heavy-based saucepan place the oil, onion and garlic and gently sweat for a few moments.

Add the apple, stir and continue to cook gently until the onion begins to soften and smell delicious.

Add the cabbage, cloves and a splash of vinegar. Season to taste with salt and pepper.

Cover with a lid and cook gently, stirring occasionally. A little water can be added if it seems too dry. Cook gently for approx. 20 mins minimum (but it can be gently cooked for longer). This dish can also be braised at in the oven at 150°C (300°F, gas mark 2) in a heavy cast iron casserole for 3 hours.

TIP

Leftovers can be refrigerated for a few days and eaten cold as a salad, or used as you would a chutney or similar in sandwiches.

ESCALOPES DE VEAU AUX OLIVES
ESCALOPES DE VEAU CHASSEUR
145

9 Wine and roses

Life at Picardy is not all 'wine and roses'. Although most of the time we feel blessed to live in this arcadia there are darker sides too. Some species of bird, wombats, feral deer and the odd wallaby can wreak havoc in the garden. Kurrawongs are pests in the vineyard, swinging on the nets, poking their beaks through until they make holes. This lets in other little birds which, with one peck, can spoil the berry. We carry on like dervishes, shouting and sounding hooters, but they remain unperturbed or fly off into the trees and wait until we go away.

One year I arrived on Christmas Eve from Melbourne, laden with presents and food, and opened the door to a nightmare. The house was full of starlings flying around in a panic and beating against the windows, and the floor was littered with bodies of those that had succumbed. There was a rustling in the woodstove in the kitchen and I opened the firebox door and more birds flew out. Bonbon the Dachshund nearly went mad with the joy and the excitement of it all. In the sitting room the open fireplace chimney was full of fluttering wings. On closer inspection I found dead birds in bookshelves, behind cupboards and chests of drawers, and every horizontal surface was covered with droppings. A scene worthy of a Hitchcock movie. We deduced that the starlings, which fly in formation in huge flocks, swooping and turning as one, must have followed each other like lemmings down the chimneys. A little chicken wire over the chimney pots has prevented this from happening again.

Wombats love to rootle in lawns, digging and scratching and leaving putrid scats as calling cards, which dogs just have to roll in. They have dug deep burrows in the olive grove which they return to again and again, despite us filling them with prickly prunings and lawn clippings. Along the creek banks they have a city of burrows, and we have come to accept that we are the interlopers in their territory.

Feral deer have become a problem. Since deer farming has become uneconomical some farmers have released their animals as a way of solving their problems. The first year we were here I looked out of our bedroom window early one morning to see a family of three deer. Father deer had a full set of antlers, mother a smart red collar and Bambi was adorable. We were enchanted ... until we did our morning rounds of our young apple trees! We rang a few deer farms in the area thinking they must have escaped, but nobody

wanted to claim them. This obviously was not an isolated incident, and now the forest surrounding the reservoir is full of them. As more tree planting takes place along the creeks, corridors of habitat and cover for deer is increasing. Shooters can get licences to hunt in the reservoir area, which indirectly has caused another problem: wild dogs. Often the hunters only take the antlers and leave the carcasses, the dogs feed on the carcasses, become stronger, breeding increases and consequently small wildlife and farm animals suffer.

Foxes are a threat to free-ranging poultry, newborn calves and lambs, but they do keep the rabbit population in check. We have found that foxes enjoy a varied diet, starting with the cherry plums, peaches, fallen apples, grapes and finally the persimmons and any bird that isn't paying attention.

The wildlife with which we share this land and which we dread most are snakes. Because of the proximity of the creek, the reservoir and the environment we have created, tiger snakes and copperheads are a fact of life. Every summer we have several sightings near the house, and probably for every one we see there are many more. I could fill a small book with my snake stories, but I won't. They are a protected species. We hate them but we have to live with them.

Bushfire, another force of nature, is also a summer concern. We are always very happy when the long dry grass is cut and baled for hay, but we are still on tenterhooks when strong north winds and high temperatures are forecast. Although not directly affected when the last big fires were in our area it was still too close for comfort.

Early that day the temperature was 45°C and the wind ferocious. As a precaution (because they are highly flammable) we decided to pull out lavender bushes and cut back climbing roses growing near and on the house. The heat was intense and we both kept dousing our heads under the water from the garden tap as we worked. We made the decision to return to Melbourne, as we were not equipped to fight a fire, taking with us anything irreplaceable and that would fit in the car. Everything else that I treasured I photographed. We are lucky; we have a bolthole in Melbourne. Friends who stayed have told us that it was as black as night at 4 p.m. and terrifying. They began to be under ember attack, and they decided to evacuate into the local town. A decision had to be made about what to take with them. Mr E. has an extensive and much-loved library of books – he began throwing books willy-nilly into a wheelbarrow. His wife tells the story: 'Books were overflowing the sides of the barrow as he struggled in the heat, wind and smoky darkness to wheel them to the car. He was about to make return trips for more books. I yelled at him: "Do you want to stay and die?"' He reluctantly left his books behind and went into town to the football oval. Fortunately the fire kept its distance, and the library (and its owner) survives.

When we returned to Picardy the next day the walls and windows of our house were black with smoke and the interior reeked. There was a lot of burnt bark, black twigs and leaves littering the garden. We learnt that a neighbour had patrolled our paddocks regularly during the night with a pump and water on the lookout for spot fires. Sheltering in our crab apple walk was a flock of black cockatoos, which normally we only see flying past. We were happy for them to strip the trees of the green apples.

Often in these times of panic and fear funny things happen. A friend agisted cattle on a property in our road. Apparently there had been a lightning strike at the property during the electrical storm that ultimately put out the big fire. A passing neighbour had seen the strike and the small fire that started as a result, and had been able to put out the flames with his fire-fighting equipment. On checking her cattle the next day our friend discovered that the fire was still smouldering. She came to us to borrow buckets and we went with her to investigate. The smouldering fire was more extensive than she had thought, and we decided that we should contact the fire brigade. Two men were sent out to check it out, and we followed them into the property, keeping a short distance behind them. They hopped out of their vehicle and stood with their backs to us, legs astride. It dawned on us exactly what they were doing. 'It can't be much of a fire if they think they can put it out like that!' we thought. We smothered our slightly hysterical laughter and approached the men, thinking that we had called them out unnecessarily. They later explained that it was a duff fire and quite dangerous as it burns slowly and spreads under the grass and only needs wind to ignite it. A fire tanker attended, and that was the end of that day's excitement.

ON THE BRIGHTER SIDE

The life we have made for ourselves at Picardy is certainly a good life. We love our rural outlook where the changing seasons are marked by silage cutting, haymaking, fertilising and cultivation in our neighbours' paddocks. The year begins with a summer-borrowed landscape of burnished gold paddocks where the hay has been cut, interspersed with green where the pasture has regrown. Dotted around are cylindrical bales of hay. It is

never completely brown here and even in high summer there is a faint tinge of green, rather like the outside husk of an almond. In late summer we net the grapes to protect them from marauding birds and the white-veiled vineyard takes on a ghostly look. The garden at this time of the year should really be out of bounds to visitors as watering is difficult and black spot invades the roses, although dahlias and zinnias thrive.

Autumn rains bring the break of the season and almost immediately the land responds like a second spring, with the grass growing fresh and green. The garden also reacts to the rain with many of the perennials having a fresh flush of flowers, and the leaves of deciduous trees and the vines begin to wear their autumnal clothes.

Our winter outlook is green, but in the cold temperatures the grass does not grow and cows queue up to eat from lines of silage or hay on a daily basis. Cold nights can turn the garden into a white winter wonderland and when the sun shines everything sparkles and glitters briefly, before the frost melts away, and is usually followed by a crisp, clear day. In the garden it is a time to prune, weed, take stock and plan how everything is going to be more under control next season.

Spring comes with a rush and the growth of the pasture is amazing. Grass which has been close-cropped soon can be seen rippling in the wind, and it is not long before plastic-wrapped bales of silage appear. This year smart striped black-and-white plastic-wrapped bales gave the countryside our very own sculptural installation, just like the columns in Le Jardin du Palais Royal in Paris.

In the vineyard a froth of new lime-green leaves appears on the top of the twisted stocks of the grapevines. I always imagine they are a chorus line of dusky dancers in green tutus relaxing at the barre after an energetic class.

The bulbs, eagerly anticipated and welcomed, announce the arrival of spring in the garden. The first to appear are clumps of snowflakes (*Leucojum aestivate*), followed by jonquils and daffodils, and lettuce-green leaves sprout on the deciduous trees. Later in spring the roses are at their best, covered in blooms, drenched with perfume and without any sign of the dreaded black spot.

Twice every day in our neighbours' paddocks, whatever the season, as regular as clockwork, black-and-white dairy cows walk up and down the hills in crocodile lines to be milked. Every day they eat out a fresh paddock. Closer to home, the agisted beef cattle on our property graze contentedly on the grass as they move as a herd through the paddock. They have their routines too: water-trough time, quiet contemplation and

cud-chewing time, and every now and then a skittish gallop around just for the hell of it. They are very curious and line up at the fence to keep an eye on what we are doing, and enjoy a good forage in any green waste we may throw their way.

One of the highlights of living in open countryside is the constantly changing skyscape. Sunrises are always beautiful. In midwinter the sun appears late over the hills, and from our bedroom windows we watch the first rays hit our neighbours' sheds and then gradually creep across the paddocks until they light up our property. Day by day, dawn occurs earlier as the days grow longer and the sun tracks further to the south. If there are clouds the sky can be coloured red, pink and gold before the first rays of sunlight appear. When I was child this time of day was little dawn, when mists rise above the creek or when fog fills the valley, creating magical effects.

The favourite time of day for us is late afternoon. We cannot see the actual sunset to our west because it is screened by tall gum trees along the roadside, but the grassy hills to the east are flooded with intense yellow light, almost as if backlit like a stage production. The colours of the hills and the leaves on the trees seem brighter, clearer and purer than at any other times of the day. It is especially beautiful if the weather is stormy. The sky becomes a deep purple, and depending on the time of the year there is a wonderful contrast with the round hills – in winter viridian green and in summer gilded with gold. After rain sometimes we are lucky to see, for a fleeting moment, double rainbows spanning the sky. A picture just waiting to be made into a thousand-piece jigsaw puzzle.

The night sky has constantly changing effects. The waxing new moon hangs like a cheese paring, and the stars seem especially bright in contrast to the inky sky. When the moon is full our landscape of hills and paddocks is washed with a silvery light and magpies sing all night as if it is day.

One aspect of living in the country which we do appreciate is silence. Except for farm machinery working in the paddocks, an occasional dog barking in the distance, the moo of a cow or the bellow of a bull, birdsong and the odd aeroplane passing overhead, there is no noise. A granddaughter, aged four, remarked one day while sitting at the kitchen table eating lunch, 'Mama, I can hear the quiet!'

ENTERTAINMENT IN FEATHERS

Our hens, Les Mademoiselles, provide us with a good deal of entertainment, with each one having a very different personality. We would love to let them free-range more often but this particular lot are wanderers and scratchers and love nothing better than to get into the garden to do a bit of cultivation and rearranging. The background sound of happy hens talking to each other and then the loud cackle to announce they have done their duty is very comforting. I miss having a rooster crowing at dawn, but I think this mob of hens are a lot of bolshie feminists and too set in their ways to accept a man in their midst.

The small birdlife is also a constant source of pleasure. Brilliant blue wren males and their dowdier wives flit through the garden, disappearing into lavender bushes and swinging on roses that grow near the windows. The males are very jealous little men and in the breeding season throw themselves at their reflection in windows for hours on end. Their wives may be more sombrely dressed, but what flirts! – provocatively twitching their tails as they hop about.

Willy wagtails seem to like the vineyard, and fantails and Eastern spinebills feed on insects or forage for nectar in the shrubberies. A shy grey shrike-thrush nested in The Duckhouse this year, coming and going through the heart in the window shutters and successfully raised one baby. Swallows swoop at dusk catching insects, and a pair makes their mud nest every year in the covered walkway between the barn and the potting shed. Occasionally we see a red robin, said to be a sign that they have come down from the mountains because the cold days of winter are imminent. At certain times of the year flocks of firetails and bush canaries visit. Sparrows are not quite so welcome as they feed constantly on the Mademoiselles' laying pellets. Blackbirds have increased in numbers and earn their place by eating snails. Their song in the evenings is also delightful.

Slightly bigger and bolder are the magpies. In spring a group of twenty to thirty took up daily residence in the vineyard. It seemed to us that they were like a bunch of teenagers hanging out, with a lot of attitude being shown: mock fighting, almost wrestling, swooping and mucking about, generally acting like larrikins, showing off and having a good time. In the afternoons they gather in groups and have a jam session, warbling away as only magpies can. We presumed the parents were off busy with this year's crop of babies.

Bower birds visit from time to time. The female has bronzy dull-green plumage and the less-often-seen male, an iridescent blue-black. A male has built a bower of dry grasses in the dogwood walk with a little collection of blue – blue Easter-egg foil, biro tops, a peg and blue twine.

Although parrots can be damaging, especially in the apple orchard, we forgive them because we have more apples than we know what to do with and they are so cheeky, comical and colourful. Their cousins, the white cockatoos, have begun to appear with their raucous screeching and I am not so happy to share with them. The black cockatoos rarely visit us but fly lazily overhead, laconically calling to each other at dusk, heading home to the forest.

Kookaburras send the little bids into a frenzy, but who can resist smiling when they chortle and laugh? They perch on the posts in the vineyard pouncing with uncanny accuracy on anything that moves in the grass, sometimes stabbing into the ground with their sharp beaks and emerging with wriggling worms. When eagles silently soar and swoop, majestically working the air currents high above, all birds become agitated. Magpies in particular chase and harass them, sometimes following them high into the air and for long distances before returning to their territory.

10 The planning department

A lot has happened in our lives over the twenty-five years since we arrived here, and a lot has changed at Picardy too.

To begin with the garden was very one-dimensional. From upstairs the layout and spaces were very obvious. It was like looking down at a flower-filled plan. With time roses and shrubs began to grow up to form the walls of our garden rooms. This has now created a series of secret spaces leading from one to another.

The biggest change has occurred as trees have grown and matured. We have been amazed at the growth of some of the trees. Oaks and elms, which we always thought of as slow growing, are now very big trees with substantial girth. The garden is shadier now and planting will have to change to accommodate this. Some of our roses are getting old and woody, and we are faced with making hard decisions about some shrubs which have exceeded the space we originally allocated them. I guess that is the joy and sometimes the frustration of gardening – nothing ever stands still – it is all constantly changing and evolving.

My style of gardening has changed over the years and has become more naturalistic. I am not a 'rare plantswoman' and like plants that are easy to grow and manipulate into Impressionistic pictures. I also like plants that when left to their own devices self-seed, which means that the garden has an untidy time while waiting for the seeds to set. Sometimes I am amazed by nature's happy accidents and surprise – combinations which I would never have thought of which nevertheless work beautifully together. Plants that are happy to arrange themselves include many varieties of poppies. Linaria or toadflax with spires of delicate pink, mauve and white flowers and the taller spires of foxgloves in similar shades. Herb Robert, a member of the geranium family, quickly fills spaces with burgundy stems, ferny green leaves and small single magenta flowers. Centranthus, also known as valerian, or even prettier, kiss-me quick, in shades of red, pink and white, is a hardy plant that pops up here and there comes again if cut back after the first flush. Aquilegia, also with the charming nickname of 'Granny's Bonnets', turns up all through the garden assisted by me shaking the dead seedpods around in any bare spots. Sweet peas now also appear from year to year and grow much more successfully than the ones I plant. Violets and forget-me-nots are everywhere. Many rambler roses have also

seeded, and I allow them to scramble up trees and over shrubs. They are mainly spring flowering and can be cut back drastically after flowering and will return with vigour the following year. One particular rose has trusses of buds that never develop into flowers. They remind me of the old-fashioned artificial flowers which were used to trim hats. I have named her 'Sunday Bonnet'.

Every winter I worry that the beds looks empty, and every year the miracle of spring occurs and the garden fills again with flowers.

Hedges play a very important role in keeping structure to this more relaxed style of planting, and the care and maintenance of them is in Bryce's department. Our gardening partnership is as follows: Bryce is in charge of the control side. He likes the garden to be neat. His idea of gardening is to take things out. His forte is the hedge clipping, grass edging, the hand mowing and of course the vineyard and a lot of weeding.

We share the ride-on-mowing and I supervise his pruning.

My department is the planning. I like the ambience of the garden to be romantic, whimsical and filled to overflowing. My idea of gardening is to put things in. My duties include the care of the roses, the cutting back of perennials, choosing and planting the vegetables, annuals and bulbs. Mostly it works.

If we had our time again there are a few things we would do differently. We would not plant twenty varieties of apples – too much fruit – and we would prune and shape the trees much harder in their formative years. Paths would be wider – we planted too close to the edges – not allowing room for growth. We underestimated the size of shrubs when they mature – we had never stayed long enough in any of our other gardens to learn that lesson.

We began our time at Picardy, twenty-five years ago, as weekenders. My weekends gradually stretched to four days here and three days in Melbourne. To make all this possible Bryce worked in the city, driving to Picardy every Friday after work, toiling in the garden all weekend, getting up with the sparrows on Monday morning and driving back to Melbourne. He did that for twenty years until his retirement. Our plan then was to reverse our living arrangements and spend weekends in the city and the week at Picardy. However, our life now is firmly centred on this little farm in West Gippsland. Retirement, for Bryce, has not eventuated as he is still working a 9–5-hour day (albeit now in the garden and vineyard).

Our petite maison of two up and two down with a very basic bathroom downstairs served us well as weekenders but now we are permanents – not quite locals yet! – we felt a little cramped. Common sense says we should be downsizing but instead we have

extended the house. Both Bryce and I were concerned that enlarging the footprint of the house by a third would spoil the feel and scale of our small cottage, yet by building again in rammed earth, sourced from the same quarry, the two parts of the building blend together. We now have a bigger living space downstairs and upstairs a library, bathroom and new bedroom.

The sitting room is a light-filled space with wonderful views of the garden and the backdrop of green hills. It has the feeling of a conservatory, or in my more fanciful moments, *une salle de jardin*. The bedroom upstairs overlooks the pond rose garden on one side, into tree tops and the vineyard on another and has French doors opening to a Juliet balcony. I plan to grow climbing roses to grow up and entwine the wrought iron balustrading. Removing established roses to make way for the new extension took place in the middle of summer. We pruned them back severely, heeled them in elsewhere and watered them frequently. They immediately put on new growth and settled into their temporary home happily. They have since been through the same process when they were shifted once more to their new positions and are now covered in buds. Roses are the most hardy and accommodating plants.

Living in situ while a building rose around us has been an experience, with work beginning at 7am and in the 'Rammers' case sometimes working until after dark. We have been blessed with wonderful tradesmen who have taken great care, under difficult and cramped conditions, not to damage the garden and have built us a beautiful home.

We find it hard to believe that we have been here for a quarter of a century – longer than anywhere else we have lived. Our three children have been married here and now have families of their own. We have buried four loved dogs, one cat, a duck, a horse, a sheep and quite a few chooks. From bare paddock beginnings together we have made a home and a garden which we love dearly. We have welcomed visitors on Open Days – we have visitors who return every time the garden is open, and it is lovely to meet them again. Tour groups have also visited from South Australia and Queensland, and recently we had an inquiry from Russia!

We never set out to make a show garden but it gives us pleasure to share it with others and we hope to continue gardening and living at Picardy, our little French folly, for many years to come.

Acknowledgements

I would like to thank Kay Scarlett and Clive Hebard of Bonnier Publishing Australia for their kid glove handling and encouragement of a first time author; Sue Stubbs for her beautiful and evocative photography; Sue Viccars, the copyeditor who made my glugs of oil into tablespoons; and Tracy Loughlin the book designer who has put it all together so beautifully.

Also thank you to all the craftsmen who have worked on the *petite maison*, the barn, the new extension and landscaping. I appreciate their patience and skills in making my dreams and schemes into reality.

A special bouquet of thanks goes to Janelle McCulloch who visited Picardy on an 'Open Garden Day' in November 2016. She introduced herself and I discovered that she was the author of *Paris: An Inspiring Tour of the City's Creative Heart*, a book which we had used to find our way around the *arrondissements* of Paris. Very quickly it was established that she was not only a Francophile like me but also an ardent rose and flower garden lover with an interest in architecture and design. Despite a significant age difference Janelle has become to me both a mentor and a wonderfully generous friend and without her encouragement and chivvying this book would never have been written.

Finally my heartfelt thanks go to my husband Bryce who has been my partner and co-creator in our houses and gardens over the years. Without his support and hard physical work, my life's work, Picardy, would never have been achieved.